ARE YOU FUN TO LIVE WITH?

ARE YOU FUN
TO LIVE WITH?

by Lionel A. Whiston

WORD BOOKS, Publishers
Waco, Texas—London, England

Grateful acknowledgment is made to the following for permission to use copyright material:

The Division of Christian Education of the National Council of the Churches of Christ in the U.S.A.

Quotations from The Revised Standard Version of the Bible, copyright © 1946 and 1952.

Cambridge University Press

Selections from The New English Bible: New Testament. Copyright © 1961 by The Delegates of the Oxford University Press and The Syndics of the Cambridge University Press.

Library of Congress Catalog Card Number: 68-31118

Printed in the United States of America

To my wife

FOREWORD

This book has grown out of retreat and small group experiences of recent years. It is an attempt to implement the Christian faith in the area of relationships. The emphasis is on *how* one can apply the principles of communication which are integral to the Spirit of Christ and to the deepest desires of human nature.

The illustrations are taken from life. They are real stories of real people, though in some cases the names have been changed. If it seems that success stories predominate, it should be stated that my purpose is to show that faith *does* "work" and that human nature *can* be changed. Miracles take place so often that one can only stand amazed. On the other hand, it is certainly true that there are times when one must hold fast in faith in apparently "unsuccessful" circumstances and situations.

Many friends have encouraged me and have been extremely helpful in the preparation of this book. I am grateful to Easter Straker, Dale Fair, Bruce Larson, Richard Engquist, Priscilla Houghton, Bruce Van Blair, Phyllis Bailey, and to my children and grandchildren, some of whom read parts of the manuscript and made helpful suggestions. My wife has been of great help throughout the preparation of the book.

LIONEL A. WHISTON

Wrentham, Massachusetts
April, 1968

CONTENTS

INTRODUCTION

Lee Whiston is a minister in the New Testament tradition—life-centered and people-oriented. He is also my friend, and a partner in mission.

Hundreds of men and women, many of whom I know personally, have found faith and freedom and the love and power of God through Lee's ministry. Since his retirement as a New England pastor he has been much in demand as a conference speaker and retreat leader. Now this book will extend his ministry to many more people, and for that I am grateful.

Three things are likely to happen to the reader of this book. He will discover God in new ways. He will find new dimensions of his own needs and also of his own potential. And finally he will learn new ways to communicate more effectively by word and action with those who make up his world.

The author believes that God speaks to people today—speaks to them by name and about specific situations. He suggests ways by which we can learn to listen to God expectantly—practical ways drawn from his wide experience. He further believes that men and women of faith can and must learn to communicate relevantly with those about them, and that this communication has to do with absolutes and with The Absolute.

These two concerns are at the very heart of Lee's book. What could be more pertinent or more timely?

I thank God for this book and for the author, and commend it to a large and varied group of readers searching for life and authenticity in our time.

BRUCE LARSON

New York City
April, 1968

Joe Mills knelt at the altar rail in his church. In the moment before the pastor approached with the bread and wine of the Communion service, Joe prayed silently, asking how he could dedicate his life more truly to God.

The thought flashed through his mind: "What about the peanut brittle?"

Shocked by the incongruity of the notion, Joe thought, *Be serious, God; I'm asking how I can dedicate myself more completely to you.*

"What about the peanut brittle?"

In the Mills family it was traditional for one of the children to go to the candy store on Friday or Saturday and buy a bag of peanut brittle or gum drops as a weekend treat. Joe and his wife liked candy as much as their three children did, but, not wanting to "overdo a good thing," they had established this custom of a modest Saturday splurge.

The candy was for everyone; it was ceremoniously placed in a dish and passed from one member of the family to another. No one was expected to dip into it alone. In fact, if one of the children was discovered taking a piece "on the sly," he ran the risk of being denied this treat the following weekend.

But Joe had fallen into the habit of regarding himself as "above the law" where the candy was concerned. After the children were in bed on Friday night he'd often find his way to the pantry and satisfy his sweet tooth with a piece or two of "forbidden fruit." To be sure, he knew he wasn't playing fair with the family, but he would pacify his conscience with such rationalizations as: "Well, who paid for it?" or "Who made the rule?" or "Nobody needs that bit of extra energy more than I do."

When Joe got up from the altar rail he tried to think about something else, but the peanut brittle stuck to his mind as it stuck to his teeth. By the time he got home from church he knew he would have to confess to his cheating, and he determined to do so right after dinner.

Surprising, how difficult it was for Joe to admit his crime to his teen-age sons and ten-year-old daughter! Still, as he stumbled through an awkward confession, he comforted himself with the thought that one of them would come to his rescue with, "That's okay, Dad. You work hard and you have a right to favors like that."

Unfortunately, no one spoke up, and in the silence Joe felt like a condemned prisoner waiting for the judge to pronounce sentence. Nothing much was said. When the children had gone out and Joe's wife was in the kitchen, washing dishes, he thought to himself: *That's the end of that.*

But it wasn't.

A few days later Joe and his wife were taking advantage of the late-evening quiet to catch up on some reading when they heard sobs.

"That's Ruth," the mother said. Going to her little girl's room, she found her with her head buried in the pillow, trying to stifle her sobs. Joe came and sheltered Ruth in his arms, and after a few moments the youngster regained control of herself.

"Now, whatever is the matter, Ruth?" he asked.

"I'm the thief," she sniffled.

"What thief?" he said in astonishment. "What did you take?"

"The cake."

Joe's wife raised her eyebrows and shook her head in bewilderment. "What cake are you talking about?" the father pursued.

"The chocolate cake!" More tears.

The *chocolate* cake! Suddenly, everything made sense.

Months before, on a Saturday morning, Mother had baked a large chocolate layer cake, iced it, and put it on a plate in the refrigerator. That evening when she began to prepare dinner, she found that the cake was missing. So was the plate. They had completely disappeared.

"Don't look at me, Mom," said the older boy. "I saw the cake, but I thought you were taking it to a church supper, or something."

His brother's denial of guilt was equally vehement. "Sure, I thought of taking a piece—but I didn't dare."

Little Ruth's plea of innocence was most persuasive of all. "Mama, I know you're trying to teach us to be good like Jesus, so I didn't touch it."

The parents concluded that it was another piece of mischief on the part of Junior Markham, the "pest" who lived across the street. They chalked up one more black mark against that boy and considered the matter closed. And now, months later, here was Ruth admitting that she had taken the cake.

"But how? Why?" Joe said, mystified.

Ruth sobbed out her story. She had wanted to give a party for her girlfriends, and she had taken the cake and a bottle of ginger ale out of the refrigerator. What remained of the accused of being a "glutton and drunkard." He went where the action was, sensed the interests of human beings, and talked their language. The way he acted, the words he used, the places he went were largely determined by the needs of people. But God determined his motivation and message.

Jesus' parables were addressed to common people. Their language is "non-religious" and "non-ecclesiastical." He seldom quoted the Scriptures. He didn't invite people to join him in the synagogue on the Sabbath.

Instead, he spoke in secular terms—of sowing seed, looking for lost money, hiring laborers, tending sheep. He used illustrations relating to the ordinary mentality and to ordinary human problems.

However, when he was with his disciples, who were deeply committed men, or with the scribes and Pharisees, who were religiously-oriented people, he often quoted Scripture and spoke of God. Again, his method and manner were determined by the needs of people.

When Jesus was with people the greater flow of dynamic power in the conversation and action was always from him to them. They might find him offensive, or attractive. They might ignore him, or change their way of life because of him.

Zacchaeus extended his hospitality to Jesus for a single meal, and as a result of that encounter he promised to give half of his goods to the poor and to make four-fold restitution for past wrongs. Picking up the "tab" for that meal cost Zacchaeus plenty in one sense, but in another it yielded extraordinary benefits!

As Jesus moved among men he did not demand homage because of his position, but renounced his prerogatives and status (see Philippians 2:6-8) and humbled himself, becoming the servant of all, vulnerable and defenseless, even to the extent of hanging on a cross.

It was this very quality of defenselessness that made him approachable. People came to him, and in coming they found their heavenly Father. Jesus' assertion, "I am the way . . . no one comes to the Father except through me" (John 14:6), is not a piece of crass egotism. He was saying that he embodied the eternal principles of communication whereby people walk into each other's hearts and into the heart of Reality. Whenever people are honest with each other in costly love, they are drawn close to each other and they reach a new depth of reality. "Wherever two or three are gathered together in my name" (that is, in love and honesty) "there am I in the midst of them" (that is, there is the sense of the presence of God) (Matthew 18:20).

The Incarnation—Christ's coming to earth in human form—is God's master stroke of communication. This communication is duplicated (or at least echoed) whenever men are willing to be transparent in love with one another, laying down their lives in costly openness, and becoming vulnerable. Others can then walk into the hearts laid open for them, and enter into the presence of God.

They can, of course, repudiate this vulnerability, be indifferent or even hostile to those who have laid bare their lives. Wherever there is loving self-disclosure, God is set free in the hearts of men, to be rejected or accepted, thus the doctrine of the Incarnation leaps to life in our midst today.

Just as two thousand years ago in Jesus, God seeks men in whom he may live and through whom he may reveal his love and his reconciliation. God calls us to be people through whom he can communicate to his other children.

Our language, manner, and the mode of our lives may be determined by the needs of those around us, but it is God's love in us that determines the spirit of our lives. He breathes his love into us and seeks to motivate us with the same Spirit that was in Jesus Christ. Christian communication is God's love channeled through one human being to another, interpreted in terms of the interests and understanding of the one who is in need.

QUESTIONS FOR DISCUSSION

1. What, to you, is the difference between "leading from weakness" and "leading from strength"? Can you give an example of either or both from your own experience?
2. Can you suggest what are some of the elements that lead to communication in depth between individuals? Illustrate from your own life, if possible.
3. Have you ever tried to "unmask" and be open with someone else? If so, what effect did it have on you?
4. What are some of the factors that pressure one person to "pull rank" on another? How have you tried to deal with these factors?

Esther Scott got the bad news in the worst possible way. When she came home late one afternoon from an appointment with her hairdresser, she picked up the evening paper from the front doorstep, went into the living room, sat down, kicked off her shoes, and glanced at the headlines.

"Businessman Charged with Embezzlement," leaped up at her in bold black type, and there, incredibly, was Tom's name. Esther's husband was accused of embezzling $40,000.

Again and again she read it over, hoping that her eyes were playing tricks on her, looking for assurance that it was, somehow, someone else. But no; the words didn't change.

Overwhelmed with shame, heartbreak, and fear, Esther turned to God in prayer.

When Tom came home that evening, temporarily free on bail, he threw himself at Esther's feet and blurted out his story. "I've been gambling on the quiet for years, losing more and more. I didn't mean to steal from the company; I always meant to repay the money. But finally I couldn't juggle the figures any more, and today they caught up with me."

Tom's hands trembled and his voice wavered as he said, "I'll have to go to prison. You'd better get a divorce and forget about me."

Esther looked deep into Tom's eyes and said: "Listen to

me, Tom. We stole this money together. We'll go to prison together, and then we'll rebuild our lives together."

At first he couldn't understand what she was driving at. "They can't touch you, Esther. You had nothing to do with it."

Slowly she repeated her words: "We stole the money together. We'll go to prison together, and we'll rebuild our lives together."

At last Tom comprehended his wife's meaning. She was identifying herself with him, making his guilt her own. She would be his partner through the prison years, suffering, working, helping him to bear the shame, giving him hope that they could and would begin again when it was all over.

There is an Old Testament story of identification similar to that of Tom and Esther. It is the story of a husband who took the initiative in love. Years after his marriage, he discovered that his wife was cheating on him. When confronted with his accusation, she taunted him for his trusting nature, and even sneered that the children whom he adored were not his children.

With that, she left him and went to her lovers. For the husband, lonely months dragged into years, but he never forgot the wife of his youth, and he continued to long for her with every part of his being.

In the meantime, she drifted from man to man, her beauty fading, her bills unpaid, until everyone despised her. Finally, her creditors put her on the auction block, offering her as a slave in order to regain their money.

When the husband heard that his wife was to be sold, he went to the sale and bought her back.

"Stay with me," he said, "and prove yourself. The time may come when we can resume our marriage and make a new home for ourselves."

Still his heart was broken. He went up onto the roof of

his house and sat under the vines which grew there. Looking out over the city of Jerusalem, he cried, "O God, I have loved my wife these many years, but she has not returned my love. I have been faithful; she has been faithless." Through tearful eyes he looked over the city, and gradually a great truth shook him out of his self-pity.

"My God, my God," he cried suddenly, "have you been going through suffering like mine? I never thought of that before. You have loved your people Israel, but they have been false to you. They have gone after other gods. These gods have received their devotion. Your people have deceived you and played you false, even as my wife has me. How your heart must ache!"

It must have been an experience something like this which came to Hosea, the prophet. Slowly this man had been taken from his own small circle of heartbreak and plunged into the depth of despair and suffering that is in the very heart of the universe. He saw that God is a God of suffering love.

Hosea "dipped his pen into his own heart's blood and thinning it with his tears" penned such words as, "Oh, Ephraim, how can I give you up? When Israel was a child, I loved him. It was I who taught him to walk. I led (him) with cords of compassion, with the bands of love." He wrote of the steadfast faithfulness of God, of the loving concern of a heavenly Father in contrast to the unfaithfulness of a fickle people.

In Isaiah we see this kind of identification in the portrayal of the "Suffering Servant." "He was wounded for our transgressions, he was bruised for our iniquities, upon him was the chastisement that made us whole and with his stripes we are healed" (Isaiah 53:5).

This same kind of love is constantly revealed in the life of Jesus. He loved his disciples, trained them, and set them free to be themselves. Again and again they used their freedom in such a way as to disappoint him, and finally they deserted him. But he kept the channels of communication open, identifying himself with them and loving them to the end.

One gets the feeling that Jesus was never really separated from either his friends, as he taught and challenged them, or from his enemies, when on the cross he prayed, "Father, forgive them, for they know not what they do." In Jesus, we see an unbreakable bond of love and a never-ending desire to identify and communicate. This quality is at the heart of the universe and reaches out to every human being.

An artist once created a most unusual painting of Jesus on the cross. The body stood out in sharp relief against a darkened background. But as one gazed at the painting, a second figure seemed to appear among the shadows. It was as if God could be seen behind the figure of Jesus. The nails that went through the hands of Jesus went into the hands of God. The nail that fastened the feet of Jesus held fast the feet of God. The crown of thorns was somehow on God's head, too.

The artist had made clear his conception that it is through the experience of Calvary that we look into the eternal heart of God. What we see during those hours of torture is a picture of God's suffering, outgoing love.

It is not only Jesus but God himself who forever identifies with us. There is an infinite concern at the center of the universe for man, whether he be in joy or in pain. It enables him to say, "If I ascend to heaven, thou art there; if I make my bed in hell, thou art there" (Psalm 139:8).

Christians often miss this analogy of the agony in the heart of God. Rather, they picture God as separated from man's despair, looking on perhaps in sympathy but basically outside the human condition. Even religion has been seen as an escape from the problems and tragedies of life.

Suppose Esther Scott had said to Tom, "I'll be praying for you while you're in prison," or that Hosea had said to his wife Gomer, "I'll ask God to forgive you." How separating and devastating such words could have been! Often our piety sets us apart from others, rather than drawing us together. How shallow, too, is moralizing. nagging, or giving advice. These smack of self-righteousness and superiority. Jesus identified himself with mankind, and to follow him is to be willing to identify with the heartbreak and loneliness of the world. The true Christian cannot be exempt from "involvement." He must of necessity suffer and act when he is exposed to human needs.

The Atonement is God's communication with us even to the extent of personal identification with our deepest despair and guilt. Like the Incarnation, the Atonement is not only an event in history but a picture of God's eternal way of life. It is something in which we, too, are called to identify with the pain, despair, and aimlessness of men. We are to bear these burdens as though they were our own—for they *are* our own.

Esther Scott did not point the finger of scorn at her husband any more than Hosea did at his wife. What they said, in effect, was, "What is there more that *I* can do?" Esther identified with Tom in his sin, and carried his shame and loneliness as her own. Hosea bought back, forgave, and lived with the faithless Gomer, wooing her to love and loyalty.

Just so does God say, "What more can I do? Since they have beaten my servants, I will send them my only Son. Surely they will respect him" (Luke 20:9-13).

The world repudiates this approach to life. It says, "Let the other fellow change. I've done my part, now it's up to him." Where barriers arise and separate men, each one blames somebody else. In international relations this is very obvious. On the national scene it is no less painfully clear. Even in the home, parents try to get their children to change, and youth wish their parents were different.

Wherever there is a wall between us and someone else, God asks us to look within ourselves and say, "What more can I do? In what ways can I change? How can I love more wisely, identify more closely, bear another's mistakes more as if they were my own?"

Identification of this kind may cause derision and rejection. Hosea's contemporaries ridiculed him for the way he dealt with Gomer. Esther Scott's friends openly disapproved of her standing by a failure like Tom. When we identify with the outcast, the needy and the lonely, we become known as softies, do-gooders, cowards, squares, nigger-lovers, sentimental fools. Eyebrows are raised, tongues wag, and people assume we've lost our senses. True communication is always costly. It may cause a man to lose his job. It may ostracize our neighbors. It may force us to become outcasts. Paul calls this our "striving to make up that which is lacking in the sufferings of Christ" (Colossians 1:24). It is our part in "bearing the sufferings of the world."

Identification takes place when a parent truly listens to his child, when a wife suffers with, but does not nag at, her husband, when a Peace Corpsman works alongside a discouraged peasant, when one nation brings to another plows and not napalm.

Reconciliation is a slow process. We run the risk of apparent tragedy and failure, as when five missionaries died at the hands of the Aucus in Ecuador. Yet beyond the temporary failure is the way of triumph. Easter always follows the dark night of Calvary.

Communication means that kind of identification where we lay our lives down alongside another's with an unbreakable love. Such love foregoes one's own will and desires and sees the need of another, and so lives and loves that the good

in him ultimately triumphs. Jesus did this both in his living
and in his dying. God is eternally doing this, and asking us
to let him do it again through us today.

QUESTIONS FOR DISCUSSION

1. Where do we usually place blame? Why?
2. What steps can you take to enable you to identify with
   others? In your family? In social, economic, or ethnic
   groups different from your own?
3. It is said that identifying with others can be costly. What
   are some of the costs?

It was close to midnight when the committee meeting ground to a halt and the pastor wearily climbed into his car to head for home. But when he passed by the Bradfords' home he saw that it was ablaze with lights. Through the picture window, he could see Ed and Eleanor Bradford sitting in front of their fireplace.

On an impulse, and more for a lark than anything, the pastor parked his car, ran up the driveway and rang the Bradfords' doorbell. Ed and Eleanor were parishioners of his, and good friends, and he felt the need of a few moments of pleasant conversation after the exacting evening he had been through.

But when Ed opened the door, the pastor's pleasant greeting died on his lips. An almost palpable atmosphere of worry and fear hung over both Ed and his wife and communicated itself instantly.

"What in the world is the matter, Ed?"

It was Eleanor who answered heartbrokenly: "Steve's sick again . . . a bad cold, and we just know it's going to turn into pneumonia."

Steve was the Bradfords' four-year-old son. Ever since birth he had been plagued by a series of ailments: one chest cold after another, bronchitis, and several bouts with pneumonia. Winter after winter, illness seemed unavoidable, and the doctor was a constant visitor. No wonder Ed and Eleanor were fearful and discouraged.

The pastor began to speak, not about accepting the illness with good grace, but about the destructive power of fear. "People who love each other seem to be on the same wave length," he said. "They're not only responsive to each other, but they can actually precondition each other to such things as illness." He suggested that the parents' attitude was affecting their son by transferring their fear to him.

"But what can we do?" the father asked in despair.

"Every man's life is a channel, either for faith or fear," the pastor asserted. "Each day—yes, each minute—we are transmitting thoughts that convey confidence and assurance, or doubt and despair."

The Bradfords had heard these ideas expressed many times in sermons, but now they were concerned enough about their problem to consider them more carefully.

"Of course, we know Steve responds to our moods and attitudes," Eleanor admitted, "but how can we help being fearful? We've been through this so many times, and each time is worse than the one before."

"Would you like to learn how to become a channel of faith? Are you willing to begin right now with your boy?"

"Yes, we'll do anything," was the instantaneous response.

After explaining what he wanted them to do, the pastor accompanied the parents upstairs to their son's bedroom. Steve lay in troubled sleep, feverish and straining for breath.

They gently moved the little bed away from the wall, and one parent stood on each side with the pastor between them at the head of the bed. He rested one hand on each parent's shoulder, and they on his, and with their free hands the father and mother lightly touched Steve's chest. Now they formed an unbroken circle of love and prayer. Not a word was spoken.

For about ten seconds the boy wriggled and twisted, then he relaxed and fell into a deeper sleep. The three adults stood silently, feeling and believing that their bodies and spirits were channels for the healing love of God. As the pastor had suggested, they concentrated on thoughts such as these: "God, your love and healing power are flowing through us now into this little boy. We picture this love as a force permeating his whole body. We see him being made well. Thank you, God."

After a few minutes they left the bedroom. It was suggested that the parents repeat this ritual every night before retiring. Steve's being asleep was helpful, for if he were awake he might resist their touch and interrupt the concentrated "flow" of faith. The pastor believed that in sleep the boy's mind was more available to the suggestions and loving presence of his parents.

Back in the living room, they offered a prayer of thanks and assurance that the healing power of God was already at work, and then the pastor left. It was apparent that the parents were already more hopeful and assured.

A few days later the pastor stopped by at the Bradfords' to see how things were going. Eleanor said that they were continuing this form of prayer every night. "My attitude throughout the day is changing, too," she added. "I don't think and pray fearfully any more. I'm trusting and thanking God more often."

Several weeks passed before the pastor's next visit. When he asked, "How's Steve?" the mother led him to a window overlooking the back yard. Through it they could see a red-cheeked boy in a snowsuit, rolling and playing in the snow to his heart's content. Could this be the "delicate" Steve?

"This is the first time he's ever played in the snow like that," Eleanor announced joyfully. "He's perfectly well—he just seems to glow with vigor!"

So often we forget the power and effectiveness of faith! Wherever he went, Jesus radiated confidence. Time and again he said, "Fear not; have faith." He spoke of the amazing results of faith—that it could move mountains. He noted the faith of the Roman centurion, and of the woman who was healed when she touched his garment. He affirmed the power of even the smallest amount of faith—the size of a mustard seed.

Yet we who should be following our Master and living in faith frequently give expression to fear: "Every time you get in the car, I'm afraid." "I just know Jack is going to flunk those examinations." "Oh, oh! Here comes Sarah. We're in for a miserable evening!"

How often we think failure, express fear, dwell on our fatigue, and recount our ills! We are fearful and negative about people, believing and expecting the worst. Negative thinking can control us with tyrannical power, but the Spirit of Christ can defeat this attitude of mind and help us to "accentuate the positive."

Even our praying is often fearful: "Dear God, don't let this cold turn into pneumonia!" A prayer such as this centers one's thoughts on the sickness and on himself. Constant repetition of this kind of prayer makes one more and more conscious of his own condition, more and more tense, until he is so fearful that he actually becomes seriously ill. It is an established fact that real illness may develop as a result of fixating on fear.

The reverse manner of praying would be, "Thank you, God. I believe your love and power are flowing through me now. I know your healing is moving through my body." The very words of this prayer encourage relaxation. Centering on God, not self, on wholeness, not disease, is the creative prayer of faith. It opens a channel through which God's power can flow, and physical and spiritual renewal can take place.

An overly-protective mother will send her child to school with a negative suggestion: "Don't get your feet wet. Try not to catch cold." How different her whole attitude would be if she said something like, "Have a happy day," or, "God goes with you to protect you." Or, to a teen-ager, "Every time I see you walking down the street I feel so proud and thankful that I have a son like you."

Bill Clark had been in the hospital several times with a cardiac condition. His wife Dot, a nurse by profession, was frightened every time she heard the telephone ring. She imagined it would be someone from Bill's office saying that he'd had a heart attack and been taken to a hospital.

The Clarks' friends all knew about this situation, and one day one of them made a strange request. "Bill, may I come and have breakfast with you and Dot every day for a week?"

In spite of his surprise, Bill readily assented. On Monday morning the friend arrived, and the three of them had a pleasant breakfast together. When the time came for Bill to drive to work, the friend said, "I'll just stay ten minutes more with Dot, and then I'll be going, too."

Bill went downstairs, backed his car out of the basement garage, and drove along the driveway below the kitchen window and out onto the highway. Through this procedure Dot stood by the kitchen sink, clutching it tensely as she watched Bill's car through the window. When it was out of sight, she sighed deeply and turned to her friend.

"Dot, what were you thinking as you stood by the window?"

Tears came to her eyes, and she choked for a moment.

When she had recovered her composure, Dot said, "I was praying 'O God, don't let him have another attack today!' "

During the remainder of the week, the breakfast fellowship grew deeper, and the friend stayed on each morning to talk with Dot. He was able to show her that her thoughts were being transmitted to Bill all through the day. She was imprisoning him with her fear, radiating tension, virtually condemning him to further attacks.

At last Dot began to understand what the friend was telling her, and she discovered a new way of praying. By Thursday she was able to stand with her upturned hands resting lightly on the sink as Bill drove past the window. Relaxed and smiling, she prayed aloud, "Father, Bill is in your keeping today. Your love and peace are with him. I thank you for caring for him. I can let him go, and can do my work today with a calm mind."

Of course Bill's health improved. But more important, he and Dot lived more relaxed with each other. Dot did not fear for him and seek to direct him every moment. Bill, knowing that Dot had set him free, felt more at ease and lived with less tension and concern for his well-being.

Negative and fearful attitudes are transmitted, especially to members of our families, even when we are unaware of them. When payday becomes a time of tension, unhappiness, and ill-temper, with acrimonious discussion of bills and obligations, the children in a home can develop an unhealthy attiude toward money. One father of four children, aged ten to sixteen, writes: "My wife and I had a budget review and realized that we were simply going to have to reduce our costs in order to pay some long-standing medical and dental bills. So instead of 'laying down the austerity law,' we had a family conference. We laid all the figures on the table and discussed how we could cooperate to reduce expenditures. One of the girls suggested it wouldn't be right to reduce church and charity giving. All pitched in with ideas: we could save on utilities by being more careful, we could cancel a newspaper subscription, we could do without some luxuries. The outcome was a feeling of working at the problem together, and a sense of participation by the children, rather than one of being imposed upon "

A father who constantly refers to the "rat race" and the "office grind" preconditions his son's attitude toward the business world. A mother who grumbles about housework and the sacrifices of child care can warp her daughter's attitude toward the tasks of womanhood. Parents who criticize their neighbors, who have "roast preacher" for Sunday dinner, who reflect unloving attitudes toward people of other nations, races, and faiths, foster deep-seated prejudices in their children.

Bigotry does not result from facts and fellowship, but from prejudices expressed in the home.

Every person is a center of communication every day of his life. He communicates fear or faith, hostility or love, indifference or identification. He has the choice as to what kind of communication it shall be. He can react to life by adding fear to fear, radiating anxiety, uncertainty, and despair. Or he can be the center of outgoing waves of faith, assurance, and confidence of ultimate triumph.

God's men are channels for communicating this kind of victorious faith, not only in life's daily situations but also in its painful crises.

They do not *react*, returning fear for fear, hostility for hostility, heaping despair upon despair. They *act*: they are channels for the healing, "wholenessing" love of God. They radiate faith in a world of fear. They light candles in the darkness. They are focal points through whom God's love and power flow to mankind.

QUESTIONS FOR DISCUSSION

1. What single word would describe your frame of mind when you come home? When you enter a roomful of friends? Strangers?
2. Do you believe there is a flow of influence between people? If so, what determines what direction it will take?
3. What are some creative and helpful ways to send children to school? People off to work? To leave people you love behind?

The usual way to deal with mistakes or problems is to change outward behavior. But even when this can be accomplished, and a more acceptable conduct achieved, it does not always enlist goodwill and loyalty, nor build inner stamina and character. Parents frequently work for quick results in child training by insisting on correct behavior, but remain unmindful of what is happening to their children's inner selves.

Scolding, spanking, threatening, pleading, promising rewards—these may produce a changed behavior pattern, but they do not build inner resourcefulness and a sense of responsibility, nor do they help the child to develop a strong character which will be an asset as he grows up and begins to make decisions in this complex world.

When Ken Harris was a sophomore in college, he wrote home to his parents that he had begun to drink with the fellows. Ken's mother Ethel was frantic, and she said to her husband Sid, "Write and tell him to stop drinking at once."

After thinking about it a few moments, Sid replied, "No, I won't. If I forbid Ken to drink, he may stop, but it will be because I made the decision for him, not because he has come to a decision on his own."

Ethel found this reasoning very unsatisfactory. "Why

shouldn't Ken have the benefit of our experience?" she protested. "Anyway, it's difficult enough these days to get through college *sober*."

After some further discussion, the parents decided to make it possible for Ken to spend several weekends at home that fall. During those days together, Sid tried subtly to get close to Ken; not pressing for an abnormal intimacy, but giving his son numerous opportunities to talk about whatever was on his mind.

Several times the two of them went hiking along mountain trails. As it turned out, very little was said about college social problems in general, or drinking in particular, but a new friendship developed between the father and son which eased communication.

One day Sid told Ken about a member of the family who had died of alcoholism. "I have quite an affinity for alcohol myself," he admitted, "so I've decided to leave it strictly alone. Not only for my own sake, but for your mother's and yours."

Ken didn't comment on this. They resumed their climb up the mountain, and some hours passed in the deep silence characteristic of men who enjoy being in the woods. Occasionally one of them would make a comment, but what passed between them was largely unspoken.

Three months later, Ken again raised the question of drinking in one of his letters, but this time the emphasis had wholly changed. "I've decided not to drink," he wrote. "Some of the fellows in the dorm have been going off the deep end. I've come to the conclusion that drinking is wrong for me. I hope I can get some of my friends to take a good look at themselves, too."

There was nothing immediate or dramatic about Ken's change of heart. He made his decision knowing that whatever path he chose would not affect the deep love of his parents for him, nor would he lose the relationship with them that he prized so highly.

We honor the personhood of another when we appeal to his inner self and trust him to make his own decisions. Sometimes this does not seem as quick and efficient as to plan a course of action for someone we love and are responsible for. Often it does not work out as we wished it would, but we must keep our faith strong and wait for positive results.

The way of the world is to manipulate and control outward behavior, and prevent questionable behavior or harmful acts. It's easy to say to our children, "Be good; behave yourselves." It's easy for government officials to say to people who are crammed into slums and ghettos, "Don't start any riots or we'll move in with the State Guard." But is this approach really effective? Naturally we want to effect quick changes in conduct and attitude that will guarantee solutions to problems that perplex and annoy us. Unfortunately, the failure of this approach is all too evident, both in family life and on the national scene.

How much more effective it would be to take time to listen to the needs and longings of those around us, and to hear what is really being said. When we are willing to honor the personhood of another, to listen and to grant him the privilege of making his own decisions, he begins to find a new sense of identity and importance. He feels loved and trusted. He becomes more articulate. He begins to make healthy choices on his own initiative—and not by our coercion, however well-meaning we might be.

A certain fifteen-year-old boy had fallen into a behavior pattern of utter irresponsibility. His parents nagged and "rode" him incessantly, and the "trump card" they held was the threat that when he was sixteen he would not be allowed to drive the family car. The boy became more and more hostile, secretive, and rebellious.

When the parents made a new commitment to Jesus Christ and then recognized that their whole approach to the boy was wrong, they changed their attitude, asked his forgiveness, and tried to see his good points and ignore his blunders.

They told him they were going to trust him completely and "set him free," adding, "Norman, we believe that when you're sixteen you'll be the kind of fellow that we'll be glad to trust with the car."

For a few weeks Norman abused his new-found freedom. Yet his parents continued to show love for him and trust in him. They forced themselves not to nag or "preach," and gradually he found out that their new style of life was "for real." Soon he was relaxing, opening up. A warm bond developed between parents and son. They laughed together about his past threats to run away from home, and the groundwork was laid for a mature relationship in the family.

One has to treat a youth as an adult long before he is one, for otherwise he cannot aspire to and grow into a healthy relationship with his family and peers. This procedure takes faith, courage, and love. It certainly involves risk, but no more so than the dictatorial method. While progress under this method may seem slow, it is certainly more sure than under an autocratic regime.

Jesus' analogy of the vine and the branches points out the importance of "rootage" if we would have "fruitage." We do not get grapes by tying them onto a vine, but through the vinedresser's hard work of mulching and pruning. Paul writes of the virtues of "love, joy, peace," etc., as the "fruits of the Spirit." How often we are overly concerned with the ethical behavior of another (individual or group) and unwilling to take the time to establish deep relationships. Yet it is from such relationships that the springs of love and loyalty are fed which produce not a superimposed new behavior, but one which is integral to the depth of human personality.

A minister from the North was asked to address an audience of college students, the majority of whom were black. He was warned in advance that many of them were hostile and bitter. How futile it would have been for him to offer "good advice"! And arguments would only have caused them to buttress their own positions.

The minister spoke in this manner: "I have come to ask your forgiveness. My ancestors were Englishmen, some of whom were involved in the slave trade. They sold, beat, maimed, and killed your people. The 'animals' in the slave ships were not the Africans, stacked like cordwood in the holds, but *my* people, with their brutish greed and cruelty.

"You cannot forgive them. Will you forgive me for them? America is my country. Its joy and accomplishments are mine. Its tragedies and blunders are mine, too. High on the list of its mistakes is its treatment of the Negro—slavery, repression, lack of education and opportunities, white domination, ghetto conditions. These are my sins, too. Will you forgive me for these, and for public lynchings and private murders, for subtle snobbery and ostracism?"

The mood of the meeting was one which was electric with power, and yet "broken" as falling waters. One by one, members of the audience stood up to confess their bitterness, some of them even asking forgiveness of the speaker for their own hatred. New courses of reconciliation were charted that night.

Ed Kerends prided himself on being a self-made man. But this "self" was not equal to the task of managing his temper or controlling his self-indulgence. One day, "as a last resort," he tried God. With the same single-mindedness that he had applied to his business, he gave himself to God. Each morning he read the Bible and spent a few moments in prayer, getting his orders for the day from his new "Boss." For the first time he was honest with his family and admitted that his self-made man image was phoney.

"I have not been able to manage myself; I have needed a new Manager." Then he added, "Why should I think I can run your lives?"

Ed's wife and children soon discovered that these were more than empty words. Instead of being the boss in the family, he became a father-friend. Previously he had spent a good deal of time fishing, alone or with one or two cronies. Now he paid much more attention to his family, taking an interest in their activities, arranging for times of recreation together.

Needless to say, they responded eagerly to their "new" father. As time passed, a family Round Table evolved, the key to which was Ed's challenge, "I'd like us all to try the experiment of letting God be the boss of this family."

The Round Table gave an opportunity for all to express their complaints and gripes freely and without restraint. They took turns reading and commenting on a favorite book, discussing TV programs, movies, and passages of Scripture. The tasks of the coming week were talked over. Problems were discussed: allowances, bedtime, new clothes, social privileges, chores, homework, friendships. The parents learned how to speak freely about their childhood and youth, of mistakes, lessons learned, "boo-boos" they had made.

Ed would reiterate, "I'm not wise enough to know what to do about allowances, hair styles, methods of study. Let's see what each situation demands, and ask our new Boss what he thinks."

During the Round Table periods, time was devoted to silence, during which each member of the family wrote down the thoughts that came to him and later shared them with the others. Of course, at first there was some "cheating" on the new Boss, and various selfish directions were reported. One child felt he should be allowed to stay up later, another thought he should have a larger allowance, a third felt she should have the privilege of adopting an exaggerated dress style. But in time the novelty of the new freedom wore off, and if one member of the family tried to put something over on the others, the presence of five other people who were becoming increasingly honest began to have a devastating power.

Kathy at first took advantage of her "cheap" freedom, but gradually the inner leadings and thoughts that came to her were far more demanding than in the days of parental autocracy. God was asking more of her than her parents ever had. However, because the ideas that came to her were her own, and not forced upon her, she was much more willing to accept them.

Ed's wife admitted that she had insisted on the children's doing the dishes because she herself hated that chore. Now she offered to share in this task. Ed, too, began to work with his sons at home. rather than insisting that they handle all the routine chores.

It soon became obvious that each member of the family was accepting a more rigorous way of life, but liking it, and even being made ready for stricter discipline. There was an increasing desire to share in the responsibilities of the home and to "spring" happy surprises on one another. At its best, human nature responds to both increased freedom and to costly responsibility.

Another breakthrough in the Kerends family came when Ed told of Lenny, a worker at the plant who was about to be fired for absenteeism. Ed had learned that Lenny's wife was desperately ill, and the family deeply discouraged.

During a Round Table, Kathy suggested that they all visit

and befriend Lenny and his family. Soon they were involved in a relationship which was beneficial to both families. The children played together and helped each other with schoolwork and household chores. Ed's wife found a warm friend in Lenny's wife. Everyone found a new outlet for his energies and his desire to serve. And because Lenny and his family were black, while Ed and his family were white, it was a valuable experience in the art of living and of destroying prejudices.

The source of authority in Ed's household had been transferred from within the home, where human wills had constantly clashed, to outside, where each will was gradually being sublimated to God's will. Any rebellion was against God and human needs. It was hard to argue with that! As the members of the family corporately obeyed their leadings, they were drawn closer and closer together, for their "focal point" was beyond themselves.

In concern for and friendship with Lenny's family, they found a concrete way to express what was happening to them. True, some of their friends disapproved, and spoke of them slightingly as "do-gooders," but this opposition and criticism only served to strengthen the family loyalties.

A college teacher noticed that each fall a dozen or more freshmen were dismissed from the small school after only eight or ten weeks. Characteristically, they drank, frittered away their time, stayed up late gambling, and neglected their studies.

After seeing this pattern repeated several years, the teacher determined to visit the homes of some of the expelled students. To his surprise he discovered that nearly all of them were strongly-churched homes, those of pastors and church officials. In conversation with the parents he found that most of the youths had been brought up under close supervision, directed with a strong hand, with little opportunity to make their own decisions or to make mistakes. When separated from the home ties, the young men were not able to handle their newly-given freedom.

Living is an art, not an exact science. No art is developed without countless attempts and mistakes. In fact, no art is ever completely "learned." The skilled pianist is far more conscious of his own shortcomings than is his audience. In the art of living we also make mistakes, even as a child learning to walk falls often, or as a piano student hits many wrong notes. We learn both through mistakes and through the joy of accomplishment.

A sign of maturity is the facility with which we can recognize a blunder and correct our actions. Mature parenthood or friendship is to live with another so that he is given opportunity to choose, to make mistakes, to correct himself, and to feel that he is surrounded by love and understanding throughout the entire procedure.

True freedom carries with it the inevitability that mistakes will be made. No one can choose the right unless there is the possibility of choosing the wrong. Yet we must keep in mind the ideal of complete freedom, which is the goal of all mature adults, and set our children free in constantly enlarging areas of life while continuing to teach them responsibility.

Perfectionism, which is often the goal of those who emphasize correct ethical behavior, places a stranglehold on life. Children who grow up striving to be perfect often break under the strain of attempting to achieve the impossible. A high school student came home with five A's and one B on his report card. His father's reaction was, "Why did you get that B?" The same boy had weeded the garden carefully. The father couldn't find a weed anywhere, but he remarked, "Why didn't you hill the potatoes higher?"

Not unnaturally, the boy transferred the idea of perfectionism from his father to God. He grew up feeling that God was watching him at every turn to see what mistakes he made. Frequently as he grew to manhood he was afraid to initiate any action lest he make a mistake and fail to accomplish a perfect result. We are not called to perfection, but to loyalty.

There is a Bible story with an interesting example of how Jesus dealt with his disciples. James and John tried to outdistance their colleagues by seeking the places of highest honor in Christ's Kingdom. Instead of rebuking them for their unethical behavior, he appealed to their deeper and better selves.

"Are you able to drink the cup that I drink, to be baptized with the baptism with which I am baptized?" he asked (Mark 10:35-40). The question was directed toward their potential loyalties and not to their selfish behavior. In this situation it would have been easy for Jesus to moralize, to point out James and John's unbrotherly spirit, and to deliver a verbal spanking. Instead, he appealed to their better nature.

How wise of him not to emphasize their blunders, but to reach deep into the springs of being within them and bid for their love and loyalty. This is what we, too, are asked to do for ourselves and for others.

Communication can be on the surface level of seeking to alter outward behavior, or it can be in the depths as we relate to each other's motivations and loyalties. A dictator in a home or in a nation chooses the way of quick returns. His people have little or no freedom of choice. Jesus chose the slower way of enlisting men's loyalty, of loving so deeply that men became his friends and began to love him and his way of life in return.

When deeper loyalties are assured, outward behavior eventually takes care of itself.

QUESTIONS FOR DISCUSSION

1. Have you tried to get other people to change their behavior? How? Why? Did it work?
2. What steps can you take to deepen your loyalty to God? To worthwhile causes?
3. Do you keep a personal "quiet time"? Regularly?
4. Have you had experience with corporate silence in a group? If so, what are the advantages of corporate silence over a personal quiet time?

News Item: A father discovered that his daughter had spent the night with a married man. He decided to punish her by forcing her to get rid of her pet dog. Taking his daughter and the dog into the woods, he tied the animal to a tree, handed the girl a pistol, and ordered her to shoot her pet. Instead, she took the gun, held it to her own temple, and killed herself.

This grotesque incident is an extreme illustration of the lack of understanding and communication between generations. How far apart can the generations drift? Is there no willingness to understand? To listen to each other?

The generation gap seems often to be widest in the homes of parents who care. Their restrictions, preachments, punishments, and denials of privileges often bring rebellion. Parents who are trying conscientiously to do their best for their children are surprised, even shocked, when the children turn against them. Their heartbreak is proportionate to the depth of their caring.

Young people seem callous, and frequently unaware of the raw wounds within their parents' hearts, but they struggle within themselves with loneliness and uncertainty. To them, life makes little sense and values are distorted. God, the

Church, parental authority, and traditional morality are all questioned. Sometimes this questioning is covered with a veneer of gaiety, a turning to fads or drugs, or a compulsive plunge into work or study. At worst, it leads to extreme withdrawal or suicidal tendencies.

High on the list of barriers to understanding their children is the unwillingness of parents to share power. The human being is loath to relinquish power in any area of life, and in the home this can be particularly noticeable. If a man has been frustrated in his business or community life, he is likely to insist on his own way when he comes home at night. A spouse who is overshadowed by his mate consciously or unconsciously compensates by seeking to dominate his children. Uncertainty about one's ability to be a successful parent may result in his becoming very possesssive and over-protective.

A child begins his life utterly dependent on his parents, who of necessity exercise complete authority. With the passing of time, the child increasingly desires to make his own decisions. "Why do I have to do what I'm told?" is asked long before a youth enters his teens. From then on the battle of the generations is joined, as each insists on having his own way.

A parent must choose whether to bring up an obedient, "good" child, subject to his will, or to train him to recognize, and of his own free will choose, effective ways of living. Most parents, unfortunately are in the former group, wanting good children who will satisfy their egos. The subconscious rationale is something like this: "My child is good if he conforms to my will and does what I want." Power and authority are used to insure immediate results.

There can be a subtle parental pride in exacting obedience, much like bringing a dog to heel. "Good" children can be displayed, to the parents' advantage. Not only that, but they are easier to live with. Instead of arguing with their children,

parents give them a TV set for their rooms, send them to the movies, or bundle them off to summer camps in order to get them out of the way. These ego-feeding, comfort-seeking motives are monstrous, and frequently result in heartbreak.
. The emphasis in the life of Jesus was not on being "good" but on *recognizing and doing the will of God*. Parents whose discipline is directed toward raising acquiescent, obedient children presuppose that they always know what is right for their children, and demand conformity from them regardless of their inner attitudes and needs. This tends to turn the youth into an automaton who is asked to fit into some established mold—while more than likely he is struggling with inner or overt rebellion.

God seeks to establish a relationship with man which gives him freedom to make choices and surrounds him with a constant series of options between wise and foolish ways of life. God sets us free to make mistakes, assures us that he is with us in the struggle, rejoices and suffers with us, stands ready to forgive, and ever beckons us on to more and more idealistic but difficult choices and deeds.

How would this pattern of life express itself in a parent-child relationship?

Family life should be planned so that each child is surrounded with choices graded according to his ability to handle them. There should be opportunities to make mistakes which will be educative, but not serious enough to be tragic. Learning involves making mistakes, along with the faith that the child will so love life that he will continue to recognize and correct his mistakes and begin again with enthusiasm.

The parents' responsibility is to enable the child to know himself as a person, to help create situations that offer choices, to help clarify the issues involved in choosing, to enable the child to make decisions and evaluate those decisions, to give him a sense of well-being over a right decision, to instill in him a willingness to acknowledge a wrong decision, and above all to encourage him to begin again.

Recognizing a child as a person can begin early in his life. In one home after the father had given thanks at mealtime, he noticed that little Greg was gurgling inarticulately. "Yes, that's it," he smiled, "Greg prays, too." From then on Greg's babyish refrain was heard regularly at the close of the adult prayer.

A wise parent gladly lays aside his newspaper to listen to his child give an account of the day's activities. The child is accorded the right to be an individual and to have the adult's attention. All too often attention is gained only through misbehavior or ill temper.

The corollary of this is equally important: when children have had an opportunity to hold center stage, they should not be allowed to continue to monopolize the conversation, but should firmly and lovingly be told to give others a chance.

Allow a child to express his personal opinions. When little Bobby complains that his cereal isn't sweet enough, his mother should not argue with him but say, "That's right; it isn't as sweet as you would like it, but let's eat it anyway." Thus the youngster recognizes that he has the right to his own tastes and evaluations, and as he is given the chance to express his opinions—to approve or disapprove—he develops personhood. Gradually, he is allowed to share more and more in family decisions: how to spend vacation time, what clothes to buy, what kind of summer job to seek, how to balance the family budget, in which college to enroll.

At first the child is given freedom to make simple decisions, as choices are introduced gradually. "Do you want chocolate ice cream, or vanilla?" "Do you want to go to the store with Daddy, or stay home with Mommy?" The areas of freedom are enlarged with the passing years, so that by the time the child is sixteen or seventeen there can be almost unlimited freedom because the parent has made himself less and less necessary in decision making. He has prepared his child to go from under the parental roof to college, or to seek a job, as a responsible adult.

It is important not to offer freedom if you are not willing to abide by the child's choice. For example: "It's ten o'clock; do you want to go to bed now?" "No." "Well, you're going, anyhow." This destroys personhood. It is the kind of situation which is easily avoided if the parent thinks before he offers choices.

As choices become of increasing moment, counsel and wisdom are offered: "If you touch that stove you will get hurt." "If you walk where it is dry instead of in the mud, your shoes will stay bright and shiny." "Brushing your teeth means fewer cavities." This can continue through the years until it is time to talk about how to drive a car, what to do on a date and why, and what college or career to choose.

Obviously, parents must set limits within which their children can grow and discover how to make reasonable decisions. One does not give a three-year-old freedom to go out in a heavy rainstorm, or a five-year-old to cross a busy street. To grant permission to an eight-year-old to spend his allowance in any way he likes without a check-up is unwise for both the child and his parents. Instead, the father can say, "Why don't you spend it as you think best; keep account of your spending, and at the end of the week let me see your account book and we'll talk over how you've done."

Nor should a youngster be asked to make decisions beyond his emotional ability to choose. A teen-ager, for example, may want support in saying No to his friends. Charlie, sixteen, is at the phone; his friend Don is urging him to go out for the evening. Charlie has homework and wants to refuse, but he is afraid of offending his pal. A wise parent will say something like, "Tell Don I want you to stay home and study tonight." He tries to "feel" when his child needs to express something, and reinforces his position.

On the last day of vacation, Junior complains, "I hate to go back to school." It is not wise to make some such comment as, "If you studied harder you wouldn't mind," or "When I was your age I liked school." How much better is something like this: "Yes, of course you dislike going back. Sometimes I dread going to work. But the show must go on, mustn't it?"

It is well to help a child give expression to his fears or resentments by letting him know he has a right to his emotions. Then we go ahead and help him handle them, with an understanding word, a gesture of encouragement, a prayer together. "Courage is fear that has said its prayers."

As the child grows older the parent should more and more take him into his confidence so that they may decide jointly on areas in which the youth will have freedom and under what conditions that freedom is to be granted.

"Why are you and Dad always hounding me about bedtime?" Sam asked petulantly.

"Because we want you to take care of your health, and not stay up late and wear yourself out."

"If you trusted me, I'd show you I know how to take care of myself," was Sam's rejoinder.

"Would you really like it if your father and I gave you a two-week trial, if we didn't say a word about going to bed and let you choose your own time?"

"Try me."

Sam proved equal to the challenge. After the two weeks were up, his father said, "I'm proud of you, Son. Let's try it now for two months, and then talk it over again."

If Sam had shown himself to be unable to handle his freedom, his father would have had to choose between withdraw-ing the freedom and giving the boy another chance. But the parents had paved the way for handling such a dilemma by setting a time limit on the original trial.

It is sensible for the parent at first to limit the duration of the freedom period in any given area. A terminal date offers the opportunity for reevaluation and for plotting to-gether a future course. It also holds up before the child the "day of reckoning"—a very important factor to be faced all through life.

Some children make decisions easily and quickly. Others are unsure of themselves, afraid to be wrong, afraid to fail. The hesitant child must be prepared for mistakes he might make by being told this is the way he learns. He should never be upbraided for failures. Usually he is all too aware of them and has suffered inwardly.

Whenever the burden of choice becomes a threat to a child, the parent should assume the responsibility of making the decision. This may happen in an area in which the child has not been granted the privilege of making a choice, in which case the adult should decide with a firm Yes or No that can-not be changed by entreaty or tantrums, but only by the in-troduction of new factors indicating that the original decision should be reversed. Such a reversal should be done openly, with the admission that one has been wrong if that is the case, and a clean-cut explanation of the reasons for the change.

Conversation between generations is often blocked by the parents' tendency to scold, preach, or resort to "Now-when-I-was-your-age." Moreover, it is often wise for one parent to talk to the child at a time, so that he is not threatened or overwhelmed.

Parents should guard against over-protectiveness when their children make mistakes. A seventeen-year-old boy, driving with his recently-obtained license, hit a piece of ice, went off the road and damaged the side of the car.

The father, desirous of affirming his son's personhood and building up his confidence, said, "Let's go out again right now. Drive down the very street where you skidded. I know you can make it all right." When they returned from this second trip, the boy was able to articulate clearly what he had learned from the accident.

It is important what we say to a child who has made a mistake. Too often one is apt to remark, "I've told you a hundred times not to leave your overshoes on the cellar stairs, but it just goes in one ear and out the other."

One father, enraged when his daughter ran away from home to become a Hippie, said, "If I'd known she was going I would have locked her in her room."

Whether the pressure is applied with words or by force, it has surprisingly little effect on a young person. If pressure brings about a change of conduct in one area, disobedience or rebellion may occur elsewhere.

Hopefully, the stage can be set so that there will be empathy between parent and child. Pressures destroy empathy and communication. The words "right and "wrong" can be used as clubs to force a youngster into a mold. So also can Jesus, the Bible, the minister, and threats of God's punishment. Using pressures such as these may force the child into a position where he has to choose between the dictates of his conscience and what his parents want or "what the church teaches." This can have a devastating effect on his faith.

On the other hand, words like "wise" or "unwise," "effective" or "ineffective," can throw the decision back into the realm of the child's own resources. "Do you think that was wise?" "Do you think your action will prove effective?" Yet even this can be pressure, if the parent makes it so.

One crucial part of the parents' responsibility is to set before their children the issues involved in a situation, especially with reference to short-term and long-term results. For example, cigarette smoking has relatively pleasant short-term benefits. At the cost of a few cents one can have a pleasurable sensation, temporary relief from "nerves," a "lift," and a sucking sensation that psychologists tell us recalls the security and comfort of mother's breast.

The long-term results are not so pleasurable, however. One becomes a slave to a habit, more dependent on outer stimuli than on inner resources in tense situations, with a greatly increased likelihood of developing lung cancer, heart disease, and many other ailments.

In such a way, the issues of life should be set before the younger generation so that they have the facts on which to base their decisions. Opportunities should be found in some natural situation and time of empathy to talk over the short and long-term factors of such issues as cheating, petting, stealing, the use of alcohol and drugs, and fast driving. This can be done sympathetically but with candor.

Children seldom respond to working for long-term gains. They want results and gratifications immediately. Youths sometimes respond to a long-range vision. Adults, if they are truly mature, respond much more to long-term than to short-term gains. Jesus gave an example of maturity when for "the joy that was set before him, he endured the cross . . . and was seated at the right hand of God." The immediate reward of escaping death was not to be compared with the joy and reward of doing his Father's will.

A boy will practice long hours in basketball or football, undergoing fatigue and bruises, giving up recreation, and making sacrifices because the long-term reward makes it all worth while. Youths are great dreamers. They dream of making the team, winning a scholarship, becoming rich and famous. They visualize the kinds of homes and life-partners they want. Parents do well to pay more attention to feeding a child's dreams than to chipping away at his behavior.

A teen-ager wrote, "I know deep in my heart what kind of home I want, and the kind of girl I want to be, so that I'll be ready for Mr. Right when he comes along. But my father lectures me all the time. I really think he doesn't trust me. Sometimes I get so mad I say to myself, 'What's the use? I might as well have the game as the name!' "

One of the privileges attached to growing up should be the right to privacy. Everyone—adult or child—needs to have time on his own to pursue private interests. It can be tragic to hear the mother of a teen-ager say, "My daughter and I are so close, she tells me everything. She has no secrets from me." This sounds like an abnormal situation in which the mother dominates her child so completely that she prevents her maturing.

Questioning a young person about his mail, his recreation, his friendships, is usually regarded by him as "prying" and invasion of his privacy. The parents must be sensitive enough to know when not to intrude. When the youngster is in a mood to talk, that is the time for the parent to listen with genuine interest. It can be a heartwarming experience for both.

A fifteen-year-old-boy emigrated alone from England and came to live with his uncle and aunt in Wisconsin. Ruggedly independent, he earned his own way, but he was often secretive and difficult to handle. A year later, two letters arrived from England, one addressed to the boy and the other to his uncle and aunt. Because her husband was out of town, the aunt opened the letter and received the news that the boy's mother had died.

Unwilling that the youth should get this bad news while his uncle was not at home, the aunt withheld his letter until the following day. When he discovered this, he was furious, and entirely oblivious to the loving motive that had prompted his aunt's action.

He went immediately to the post office and rented a box so that he could have his own mail "unmolested." The uncle and aunt resented the boy's behavior, and a long-standing barrier arose. The adults were unwilling to ask forgiveness for violating the boy's privacy, or even to admit that they had done so. As for the youth, he did not realize how cruelly he had hurt these relatives who had opened their home to him. Nor would he admit that he knew they had acted out of love and good intentions.

This story illustrates that youth value the right of privacy, and also the necessity of keeping open lines of communication between generations.

Pete and Jane were disciplinarians, long on teaching responsibility and short on granting freedom. They insisted that their children "toe the mark." This made for an efficient, well-regulated household of which they could be proud, but slowly, signs of rebellion were evidenced. John would "accidentally" step on Lisa's fingers as she played on the floor. He took a fiendish delight in hearing his stern father reprimand the complaining daughter. John called his sister a cry-baby. There would be sly pinches under the table, and Lisa would jump and spill some food. Immediately the father would scold her, and John would smirk with a look of superior innocence.

By the time the children were in their teens their rebellion ran the gamut from polite, though unwilling, obedience by the son to open defiance by the daughter. Yet the show of respect for their parents persisted. In a way, they admired their parents' inflexibility in a world marked by softness and irresponsibility.

Howard and Sophie, on the other hand, were permissive

parents. They had started their life together in hardship. Howard had been a surveyor for a mining company, and their first home was a tent where Sophie "kept house" as they moved about the mining territory.

Then came success and phenomenal affluence. *Our children must not be forced to endure such rigors*, Howard and Sophie thought as they relaxed on their spacious veranda overlooking the sea. Cars, boats, private schools, and dude-ranch vacations were all at their children's disposal.

What was the reaction of the children of these pioneer parents? They found excitement in speeding cars, extravagant luxuries, drinking and drugs. And now their bewildered parents asked, "What's wrong with this younger generation?" Their children knew freedom, but not responsibility.

In Pete and Jane's home the source of authority was the parents. Their children's rebellion indicated that they needed and wanted to make their own decisions.

Howard and Sophie, however, who had learned discipline in their early years, thought that this would naturally be transferred to their children. They were amazed when their children became bored and constantly sought excitement in far-out behavior. In fact, the young people in this home longed for authority, and when they failed to find it their freedom turned to license. Each home must pinpoint its own needs and find its own way to fulfillment—but always there must be a dual emphasis on freedom and responsibility. Either is deadly without the other.

Parents frequently demand higher standards of their children than they are willing to accept for themselves. Convenient lies, dishonest business practices, minor law violations, income tax evasion, expense account padding, unkind gossip, and criticism are all a part of contemporary life. Counterparts show up among young people: they make untrue excuses to their friends, cheat on schoolwork, break rules. They lie about why they are tardy, use their allowances to buy forbidden articles, and deceive their parents and teachers. For these offenses parents land on their children like a ton of bricks. As for the children, they are cynical because their parents act one way and expect them to act another.

Adults talk to youth about choosing one way of life and then, unwilling to make a costly sacrifice, deliberately take another for themselves. One minister with more than fifty years of experience in pastoral work reports that out of a hundred parents who themselves smoked and who asked him to speak to their children about cigarette smoking, only one father agreed to give up the habit himself.

The current youth revolt is seen by many as rebellion against adult values which young people will not accept. The slogan, "Make love, not war," is not, in the main, an excuse for sexual license, but a demand that humanity recognize its oneness. Statesmen are more adept in the arts of war than of peace. Christianity has proclaimed the Gospel of the Prince of Peace and yet "Christians" have been deeply involved in the world's great atrocities: religious wars, the Inquisition, the slave trade, the exploitation of poor nations, the persecution and extermination of Jews, and two world wars.

Youngsters are demanding of mankind that it see all men—black and white, Communist and Christian, Vietnamese and American—as part of a common humanity. The younger generation, while often frivolous and senseless in the expression of their involvement with the negative aspects of modern life, nevertheless present a powerful symbol of youth's determination to be identified with the anguish, loneliness, filth, poverty, and misery of the world, and they are frequently motivated by genuine love and concern.

There is a seething cauldron of anger in many young people who are inflamed against the crime and graft and corruption which extends from the lowest dives in our cities to high places in government and industry. The military-industrial complex is made up of "men over thirty," men who think in traditional ways: make war, make money, amass power at any price. It is the nature of idealistic youth to hate such standards.

What many youth do not see (nor do very many adults) is the cost, the discipline, and the long-term commitment necessary to achieve peace and new social goals. They see themselves as "Bonnie and Clyde," breaking up the bastions of finance and law enforcement and introducing a new era of freedom, perhaps with the gun, perhaps with the new morality and sexual freedom, or with some other quick, easy remedy. They would like to upset a few apple-carts. But seldom do they think through the cost and discipline necessary to find dependable replacements.

Of course, there are exceptions, for example those who respond to the Peace Corps, and the increasing number who instead of fleeing the ghettos are returning to serve and help redeem them. This new breed of youth sees the long road ahead and accepts self-discipline, recognizing that peace and the new world of a common humanity can only be built by years of patient, costly sacrifice.

Peace is not merely the absence of war. It is an entity in its own right that must be built with patient care and love, with a deep desire for relationships, with a willingness to be rebuffed, slandered, and perhaps killed. Why should a man be a national hero if killed in battle, but an idealistic fool if he dies fighting for civil rights, helping to irrigate a desert in a foreign land, or teaching children in a nation in the throes of revolution and rebirth?

These are some of the things our children are trying to tell us. Is anyone listening? There is a great need for each generation to be honest and transparent, listening in love. Suppose a parent, instead of claiming to be omniscient and having the right to be obeyed, would "lead from weakness," asking his son to show him how he, the father, could bring about better understanding in the home. Suppose the Church, which to many youngsters represents the older generation, confessed its failure to teach nations the way of goodwill and peace. Suppose those of us in the Church would say with new humility, "What are the needs of the world? What has the world to teach us? Youth, what have you to say to us?" Suppose youth and adult would join hands in a common quest for Christ's way to build the new world.

Christmas is the story of a God who wanted so much to draw close to his children that he came to them in terms they could understand. He sent Jesus in human form to establish a beachhead into the human heart. When one emulates this spirit, be he youth or adult, he will find that in almost every case he can enter into a warm relationship with others, even though they are separated by a generation.

Primary in all relationships is the need for forgiveness. This is the hallmark of God, his amazing and constant forgiveness and his wiping out of the past. "As far as the east is from the west so far does he remove our transgressions from us" (Psalm 103:12). Let youth and adult alike learn to forgive, and to forget and to begin anew, not predicating possible future reactions in terms of past behavior. Paul wrote, "Love keeps no score of wrongs" (I Corinthians 13:6, NEB). Learn never to bring up the past with its errors and failures. Display a constant flow of new faith and hope in each situation, even if at times you meet with negative results.

There will always be a generation gap. It will always be difficult for different generations to relate to each other. The youth of today will be surprised when twenty years from now, they find themselves shocked and scornful of the behavior of their children. Adults should not bemoan and rebel against the situation, but seek to work in harmony, always aiming toward understanding and shared experiences.

The generations have much to give to each other. It is so easy to become cynical, bored, and jaded as one grows older, and to place an undue emphasis on security, status, and power. If the members of the older generation are willing, they can learn from the idealism, hope, and abandon of the young, with their freshness of approach, their healthy questioning of the established traditions of war, racism, sectarianism, and meaningless divisions. Wise are those adults who "have ears to hear and hear."

On the other hand, the mature person has learned to sift abiding values from those which are transitory. He has the qualities of endurance and fortitude, and he senses the priority of long-term goals as opposed to short-term rewards. The years have added wisdom and seasoned experience. Happy is the youth who will listen to such an adult. The exigencies of today need both youth and age, radicalism and conservatism, the abandon of the young and the endurance of the mature—along with the faith of both.

The fundamental stance of the God who made us is one of faith, belief in mankind even when we have lost faith in ourselves, a love that lives for us and with us even at the times when we are most unlovable. To emulate God is so to believe in the members of other generations, and so to relate to them, that our faith in them is constantly reinforced with goodwill, trust, and meaningful communication.

Questions for Discussion

1. At what stages in your life have generation gaps been most in evidence?
2. What steps have you taken to bridge the gap between

generations in your own family or circle of friends? What steps could you take?

3. What is the relationship between God's forgiveness, the acceptance of his forgiveness, and forgiveness of ourselves?

4. What has the younger generation to teach you? The older generation?

George Lewis had a problem. His twelve-year-old son, Larry, had asked permission to ride his bicycle from their home in Worcester, Massachusetts, to New York City during the spring vacation from school. George's wife was spending a few weeks with her parents in Florida, so the decision was squarely in his lap.

Larry was a lively and resourceful boy, always coming up with new ideas and breaking traditional patterns. His father was reluctant to squelch him with a quick, "No, Sir, not on your life." On the other hand, to set the boy free to go might not be in his own best interests.

George decided to "buy a little time" by suggesting a trial run to Boston, a round trip of one hundred miles, thinking that this might discourage the boy from his more ambitious plan. But Larry and a friend made the trial run without difficulty and came home in high spirits.

"Honest, Dad, I won't have any trouble," he urged. "Please say I can go."

George swallowed his apprehension and said yes. It was agreed that Larry should make as his destination the home of an aunt who lived in Rutherford, New Jersey, a few miles beyond New York. He was given the names and addresses of several friends who lived in towns along the route so that he would have someone to turn to in case trouble arose.

Larry planned feverishly for his trip. Twenty-four hours before departure time he started to load the carrier over the rear wheel of his bicycle with duffle—a full thirty-five pounds of it. George thought of the steep hills of Stafford Springs and other Connecticut towns and felt sure the boy could never negotiate those grades. But he knew that if he advised against the heavy load, Larry would insist that everything he was taking was essential.

The father was beginning to think he had made a mistake. Larry was brave, but inexperienced. The route lay along a heavily travelled highway. George sought to give over his fears to God and to entrust his son to the care of the heavenly Father.

At four-thirty on the morning scheduled for the trip, the father and son had breakfast together. When the meal was finished, they knelt in prayer. Then they went out to the loaded bicycle.

"Say, Dad, don't you think that load is a little heavy?" Larry asked hesitantly.

"What do you think?" countered his father.

"I guess I'd better leave some of this stuff behind." Whereupon the boy proceeded to take off about two-thirds of the load.

Larry reached Hartford, Connecticut, the first night, and he received a warm welcome from the director of the YMCA, who had been notified to watch for the boy. The next morning he got off to a late start, and traffic was heavy through New Haven, Bridgeport, and Stamford, so that it was past midnight when he reached the George Washington Bridge connecting New York and New Jersey.

A state trooper who saw the boy pedalling wearily along stopped him, assuming that he was running away from home. When Larry assured him that his aunt was waiting for him twelve miles away, the policeman verified this by telephone. The aunt was greatly relieved to know where Larry was and that he was safe. Her house was ablaze with light to welcome him.

Of course they had a wonderful visit. After a day's rest, Larry's aunt gave him a grand tour of New York City. When the time came for him to return home, she put him and his bicycle on the Fall River boat so that he had only a hundred miles or so to pedal home from there. There was great relief and joy in the Lewis home when Larry finally arrived at the end of his big adventure.

A few days later, George said, "Larry, I want to ask you something. I had a big struggle with myself before you left. I wanted to give you advice, to tell you of the many places where you should be careful. The reason I didn't do it was that I also wanted to set you completely free."

Larry grinned. "I know, Dad."

"Did I do right, or should I have given you more explicit instructions?"

"I'm glad you didn't," the boy replied. "I made up my mind to be as careful as possible, so you wouldn't be sorry you trusted me."

"What was the most dangerous situation you ran into?" his father pursued.

"When the big trucks went by. The first one just about knocked me over, because of the air suction. But after that I knew what to expect, and I leaned away from it."

"I'd never have thought of that," George said.

Larry went on thoughtfully, "You know, Dad, if I'd been trying to remember a whole long list of things to be careful about, it probably would have been a lot more dangerous. I'm sure you did right."

God's love is a love that sets us free. There is something

awesome about this love that "sets before us the ways of life and death" and leaves us free to choose. We are free to live in heaven or in hell, today as well as after death.

In the story of the Prodigal Son, as we find it in the Bible, the father gave his younger son his rightful share of the family inheritance. But he did not say, "You can't set foot off the property. I'll give you the money, but I'll tell you how to spend it."

Jesus set his disciples free to deny, desert, and betray him. He did not say to Judas, "Judas, there are twelve of us here. We can restrain you from keeping that appointment tonight. Sit down."

No, there was a simple, "Do quickly what you have to do" (John 13:27, NEB).

God honors the freedom that he has given us. He will not turn us into robots or automatons. He will not burglarize his way into our personalities, dictating and controlling our decisions. We hold within our persons the right to reject him, to reject reality, to reject anything and everything that we know to be right.

Of course, the laws of the universe that God has ordained are constantly at work: Judas ended up with his neck in a noose; the Prodigal found himself at the pig trough. But the ultimate choices in life are always ours.

Does this mean that if we choose to go our own way we are deserted by God? Not at all. His love follows us at all times; it actually precedes our actions. The old wording in the Episcopal Prayer Book read, "Lord, prevent (go before) us in all our doings." God does just that.

This principle is illustrated by the experience of a certain missionary who was traveling in the jungle with two guides. They spent eight days on jungle trails with many miles between villages. Whenever they came to a point where one main trail crossed another, they would find a meal, apparently prepared and waiting for them.

The missionary, new to that part of the world, was mystified, until one of the guides explained. "Didn't you hear the drums beating in the distance from time to time?"

"Yes. I hoped they were not war drums."

"Not at all. The message was being passed from village to village that friendly people were on the trail and needed food."

Just so does God anticipate our needs and provide for us in advance. He surrounds us with a never-ending love. "I have loved you with an everlasting love; therefore have I continued my faithfulness to you," God said through his prophet (Jeremiah 31:3). God goes before us, follows us, and surrounds us with his steadfast love even though we may be in a state of disobedience. His love is not conditioned by our response. It is always with us and always available to us whenever we are ready to receive it.

By setting us free, God has placed us in a position where our inner resources and responses can develop to a maximum degree. Freedom and responsible independence are essential if we are to realize our personhood and have a sense of dignity and worth.

When Henry Stevens graduated from high school he worked all through the summer and earned enough money to pay his expenses for half of his first year at college. But just before school started, Henry had an accident which put him into the hospital for six weeks and used up all of his savings.

When he was released from the hospital he was met by his only living relative, his older brother Luke. Henry had been a source of concern to Luke because of his leaping from one project and scheme to another throughout his adolescence.

"What do you want to do now, Hank?" he asked.

"Go to college," the youth replied.

"But school started six weeks ago."

"I know, but I think I can make it up."

"You haven't got any money."

"I know that, too, but I'd like to try. I can earn my own way."

Luke shook his head in frustration at his brother's obstinate over-confidence. Finally he said, "Okay, I'll give you two hundred and fifty dollars. At least it'll help some."

The younger boy stood silent, reluctant to accept the money. Luke misinterpreted his silence, thinking that Henry wanted more. "All right, I guess I can manage five hundred. Think you can make it with that?"

Still Henry was silent, embarrassed by this offer from his brother, who needed the money for his own family.

Finally Luke had a flash of insight as to the real nature of Henry's lack of response. Putting his hand on his brother's shoulder, he said, "So you want to make good on your own. Okay. I won't offer you a penny. I think you'll make out all right. Remember that I'll stand by you. If you ever need help, just call collect."

There were tears in the eyes of both brothers as they clasped hands. Henry went to college, and not only did he catch up with his class but he worked his way through to a degree without putting any financial strain on his brother. The Apostle Paul wrote, "I have learned to find resources in myself whatever my circumstances. . . . I have strength for anything through him who gives me power" (Philippians 4:11, 13, NEB).

The man who feels loved and trusted by both his fellow-man and God finds himself drawing on deep inner resources and availing himself of unsuspected hidden powers. For example, a teen-ager who is trusted by his parents is far more

likely to respond to the voice of his conscience than to all
the noble advice his relatives and friends may give him because they lack confidence in his maturity or judgment.

One can surfeit another with gifts, and one can cripple
the imagination of a child by loading him with advice. We
imprison a loved one when we surround him with posses-
siveness or fetter him with fears and grudging permissions.
God has set us free, and if we would follow in his footsteps
we must set others free.

Freedom implies the privilege of experimentation and the
probability of making mistakes. Experience comes as the result of experiment. A chemist performs experiments in his
laboratory and amasses experience which guides his future
research.

Laboratory experiments often demonstrate procedures
which should be avoided. Pasteur once said that no experiment is a failure: some teach us what to do, and some teach
us what not to do. So it is in life: as we experiment we will
make mistakes, for ours is not an automated goodness, but a
gradual growth in the desire and ability to choose the will
of God.

Many people are afraid to make mistakes. They are afraid
to fail and afraid of people's criticism should they fail. We
all need to be delivered from the fear of failure. Parents
especially need to keep this in mind, lest they unwittingly
instill a morbid fear of failure in their children. Constant
reiteration of such remarks as: "Don't do that," "Be careful
not to drop that," "I wish just once you'd bring home a perfect report card," can be devastating to a child. By repri-
manding children for mistakes far more often than praising
them for accomplishments, we keep them from learning for
themselves by their mistakes. This also breeds over-caution
and can actually create enough fear to keep people from trying new things.

Martin Luther stuns us with his peculiar advice: "Sin bravely, but more bravely glorify God." He did not mean that we are deliberately to go out and sin. But he knew human nature, and was aware that no matter how earnestly we seek to do God's will, we will make mistakes and fall short of our goals. In effect, he is saying, "Do not let the fear of making mistakes or of sinning keep you from seeking bravely to do the will of God." Our aim is not perfection- ism, but a bold, adventurous seeking and doing of God's will. We are to go ahead bravely. If we make mistakes, let us make them bravely. When we blunder, we repent, begin again, and resume our journey.

He who is learning to give up his fear of failure and his fear of criticism, and who is accepting himself as one who will make mistakes again and again, is set free to live with abandon. He has been set free by God, and he has set him- self free to live life abundantly.

Questions for Discussion

1. How can you "set free" the important people in your life? To what extent should you set them free? What does the word "freedom" mean to you?
2. What is there in you that allows others to "bug" you?
3. What are the values of acknowledging mistakes? Illustrate from your own life, if possible.
4. Discuss the relationship of freedom and responsibility.

To Alan Hartman, it looked like the chance of a lifetime. He had not been actively seeking a new job, but here was the offer. Not only did it involve a salary raise and more prestige, but added responsibility. It also meant he would be spending a lot more time away from home.

But somehow, Alan couldn't come to a quick decision about the job. He talked it over with several friends, made two trips west to investigate the company and the job requirements, and weighed the pros and cons in his mind over and over again.

Finally he went to his pastor to ask for help in making a decision. The pastor listened while Alan outlined the situation, and then asked, "How does Pat feel about the move?"

"She's perfectly willing. In fact, she's really being a good sport about the whole thing."

"Was she willing from the beginning?"

"No, at first she was against it, quite strongly, but she's changed her mind." Then he added, "She's really wonderful."

The pastor pursued the point: "Why do you think your wife was against the move at first?"

Alan thought for a moment before replying, "I'm not sure.

Maybe she figured she wouldn't be seeing much of me if I took the new job. You see, I'm quite an activist—always on the go—and we don't have much time together as it is."

When the pastor made no comment, Alan went on, "There's no doubt that the job would be a lot more demanding than the one I have now. To tell the truth, I think Pat really doesn't want me to take it."

There was silence for a moment and then the pastor said, "Alan, do you think that deep in her heart your wife is lonely?"

Suddenly Alan's apparent self-assurance crumbled. His shoulders trembled, tears rolled down his cheeks, and he sobbed audibly. When he was able to speak, he said, "I know she's terribly lonesome. I've short-changed her for years. She's been wonderful, but I give her almost nothing in return."

After the two men had prayed together, Alan straightened up and smiled the smile of a free and forgiven man. He knew now what he had to do.

The next morning the telephone rang in the pastor's study. "It's all straightened out," came the voice of a man whose very inflection suggested freedom and happiness. "Pat and I have really found each other. I see that I've just been using her, taking her for granted. But that's all over. Our relationship has come to life again, and I intend to keep it that way."

"What about the new job?"

"Oh, that doesn't seem important now. As a matter of fact, I'm staying where I am. The kids have their friends here, and my present job is perfectly all right. But I'm glad all this happened, because of what it triggered for Pat and me."

Too often we take for granted the people who are closest to us. We tend to depersonalize them by thinking in terms of what they can do for us, not who they are as persons. A man will see his wife in terms of the service and satisfaction she can give to him, and his children as contributing to or disturbing the orderliness and convenience of a household.

This attitude is frequently extended to those outside the family circle: we view store clerks and service station attendants not as people, but as automatons to wait on us. We see fellow motorists as being in our way or out of it. This age of ours classifies people impersonally as "its," as producers or consumers, as efficient or inefficient workers, as customers with good or bad credit risks. People are more and more regarded as assets or liabilities to the economic or status structure or to our personal desires.

The Gospel of Jesus Christ cuts directly across this process of depersonalization. In Jesus himself we see the ideal approach to dealing with people as human beings. To him, people were persons. The poverty-stricken widow who placed her mite in the offering box was seen as noble. Jesus stretched out his hand and grasped the emaciated hand of a leper—who had not felt the warmth of human contact and health for years. He even transformed the love people had for him into love for others. To Peter he said, "Do you love me? . . . then feed . . . tend my sheep . . . my lambs."

Perhaps the most significant evidence of the value Jesus put on people is found in his attitude toward women. In his day, women ate what was left over when men had finished. They were subject to the arbitrary commands of the head man of the house. But Jesus took notice of women, healed them of their ailments, forgave and commended them, recognized their worth. No wonder women loved him and followed him to the cross. He valued them for what they were, for their own sake, not for what the standards of the day condemned them to be.

A mother told this story with a heavy heart: "For the first

three years my son Jim was in high school I kept after him to get better grades. I nagged and scolded and urged him on. In fact, I did everything I could think of to make him double his efforts in school.

"The first report card he brought home during his senior year had all high marks. I was so proud of him.

" 'Jim, this is great,' I said. 'Let's go out tonight and celebrate.'

" 'No, Mom, I guess not,' he replied.

" 'But why not?'

" 'I'm going out with some of the fellows.'

"I was quite hurt by his indifference, and asked again why I couldn't take him out to celebrate.

" 'I don't feel like it,' he said. Then, for a moment, his apathetic look gave way to one of hostility, almost hatred, and he snapped, 'Why don't you throw a party for my report card? That's all you care about.'

"Imagine how terrible I felt when I finally realized what I had done. Because of my nagging, Jim felt that I didn't love him, but approved of him only for what he was able to do. When he had needed my encouragement, when the going was hard, I had not given a sign of love for him as a person."

A parent can be proud of a child because the child feeds his ego. An employer's pleasure in his workers can be based more on their ability to produce than in their worth as human beings. A minister may find that he favors those parishioners who attend church regularly over those who don't. The tendency in all of us is to use people and manipulate them for our own well-being, rather than to see them as individual persons and love them.

Alan Hartman, in the story which opened this chapter, had given greater attention to his problems than to his relationships. He had assumed, if he thought about it at all, that if he solved his problem about whether to take the new job, everything else would fall into place. It is a common characteristic to let problems occupy the center of our attention. We become problem-centered rather than God-centered or people-centered. Our day begins with an emphasis on things, not relationships. Our children become problems to be dealt with, not human beings to be appreciated and enjoyed.

As I began to prepare this chapter, I received a letter from the father of a teen-ager. He wrote: "My daughter has such an effervescent joy and good humor that she can lift the whole family 'out of the dumps.' What accompanies this is a carefreeness which I called carelessness. It doesn't bother her to have her schoolbooks and clothes strewn around various rooms, or to spill food on the table or kitchen floor.

"I like things to be neat and tidy. As a result, at the end of the day, even when I could appreciate her *joie de vivre*, I often found myself saying such things as, 'Please be more careful,' or 'When are you going to learn to put things away?'

"Finally it dawned on me that she was quite aware of my attitude: I had left no room for doubt, and further carping would do no good. Why should I not accept all this as part of her, and let myself love her and enjoy her, and let her enjoy herself? It wasn't easy to change, but prayer and my wife's help have worked wonders. We're all happier, and the atmosphere in our home is lots pleasanter." When the right relationship is established, a problem tends to take care of itself.

How often our first waking thoughts are problem-centered rather than person-centered! We think of the many tasks to be done, and neglect fellowship with God who offers us the necessary resources for those tasks. Our morning prayers take the form of reviewing the day's schedule rather than renewing our relationship with him who gives us the power to live victoriously through the day. It is a mistake to see life primarily in terms of tasks and obligations, not in terms of a relationship with God who gives us wisdom and the ability to perform those tasks and meet those obligations.

In Romans 12:2 (NEB) we read, "Adapt yourselves no longer to the pattern of this present world, but let your minds be remade and your whole nature thus transformed. *Then* you will be able to discern the will of God. . . ." Paul seems to be saying that if we become a different kind of person in our hearts, then, and only then, will we be able to discern God's will. This is quite different from trying to find God's will in a problem situation while neglecting our relationship with him and with our fellows. If we will first get ourselves in the right relationship with God and with people, then we will see more clearly what is the right course of action to take.

Never in history has there been such a mass attempt at communication as there is today. Television and radio assault our eyes and ears at every turn. Third class mail floods our post offices. Books, magazines, and newspapers are published in colossal quantities. Words, words, words—spoken and written by the million! Yet we know less and less about each other's inner selves. We seek to communicate ideas, techniques, programs, but keep ourselves in secret. We remain largely unknown, strangers to one another.

Our secretiveness is not necessarily planned. Sometimes we rationalize our behavior, for example labeling our stubbornness "high moral conviction," and our selfishness "looking out for my family's interests."

Even worse, we may justify our refusal to support social progress on the grounds that we must "protect property values." We shed crocodile tears over poverty and injustice, but only if it involves someone thousands of miles away.

The human impulse is to be "right" and have an edge on the other fellow. But how devastating it can be to work with or live with someone who is always right, who perpetually has to get his ideas across. We need to discover the truth that a certain wife expressed when she admitted to her husband, "I've always prided myself on being right and in seeing that my right views are passed on to others. Now, for the first time, I am beginning to see that to be always right is generally to be wrong."

Always to be right threatens and destroys relationships. The building of warm relationships creates an atmosphere in which others will listen to what is right: not necessarily the right as we see it, but as God reveals it to them.

Pastor Robinson remembers with chagrin one of the low points in his ministry. There was a motel and restaurant a few miles from the church, owned and operated by a man and his wife who were not church members. The pastor and his friends often dined there. Sometimes the church's youth fellowship used the restaurant as a meeting place.

One day the owner died. The pastor did nothing; he did not write, phone, or stop to express his sympathy to the widow. After all, this was a family outside the parish membership, and the thought that he had a responsibility never occurred to Pastor Robinson.

But a year later, when the church was engaged in extensive renovations and solicitation of funds to pay for them, the pastor offered to call on the motel owner's widow. When he spoke to her about a contribution to the renovation fund, he was suddenly pierced to the heart by the conviction that when she had been in need he had not come to her, but when he saw the possibility of getting some money for the church he became interested in the woman.

Educational processes are dependent on good relationships. We learn almost exclusively from those we love. If a history teacher is more preoccupied with dates and events than with relating to his students, it may be that they won't learn much history. If he is keen to have his students achieve in order to reflect his excellence as a teacher, then he sees them as objects to be manipulated to enhance his prowess. In this case, the student is not primarily someone to whom the teacher can relate, but someone to serve his ends.

However, if the teacher builds a warm rapport with his students, lets them feel that he is really interested in them, then they come to their classes with eager and open minds. Knowledge is transmitted when good relationships are established. This principle holds true for a home situation, with parents and children, for a church, with pastor and laymen, and for a factory with foreman and workmen.

Lucy O'Hara was a fifth-grade teacher who was having a difficult time with class discipline. Moreover, she was dissatisfied with the amount of factual knowledge she was getting over to her pupils.

One morning half a dozen boys and girls who had come early to school happened to be gathered around a new map of the world. Lucy joined them, and in a relaxed and happy frame of mind they talked about current events in various parts of the world as the teacher helped the children to locate those places on the map. There was an unusual *esprit de corps* as teacher and students exchanged ideas, asked and answered questions.

Then the bell rang, the teacher took her place behind her desk, and immediately she began to see her children as pupils who must be kept in order. Her tone of voice changed, and once again she found herself straining to impose standards in the classroom which the students must accept.

Thinking this over, Lucy asked herself, "Why can't I always have the same warm attitude toward these boys and girls, whether I am speaking to them informally before school opens, or from behind my desk? Why is there a difference in my approach? Why can't I see them as kids to be loved, not disciplined?"

It was the beginning of a new era in her teaching. The following year she had ten "problem pupils" in her class, any one of whom could have disrupted a normal routine. This was a class that teachers dreaded to have as their assignment. Yet within three months, under Lucy's regime of love and consideration, no word but "miracle" was strong enough to describe the changes that had taken place in them.

In our fiercely competitive world, in a technological age, it is perhaps natural that we tend to be problem-minded. We pride ourselves on making right choices based on data accumulated through research, computers, polls, books, and magazine articles. Material facts and human knowledge figure in our decisions, but we are often unaware of a lonely heart, a stifled dream, or a bitter spirit in someone in our own home or office. That magic moment of oneness, which suddenly makes all of life worthwhile, escapes us.

Jesus put it succinctly in two simple sentences: "Thou shalt love God . . . Thou shalt love thy neighbor as thyself." These twin commandments establish the priority of relationships. Once built, right relationships lead to genuine and abiding solutions of life's many problems.

QUESTIONS FOR DISCUSSION

1. Do you feel society making pressures on your personhood? How? How do you maintain your individuality? Your integrity?
2. What is the difference between being "resource-centered" and "problem-centered"? How do you begin the day?
3. Do you think of your home as the base and center of power for your daily life? If not, what is your center of power?

Ralph and Barbara Blank's hearts were wrapped up in their young son, David. All through his life they had seen him with the eyes of love and hoped for the best; therefore they were totally unprepared for the doctor's verdict.

"There is really nothing to be done," said the medical man gently. "Because of David's brain damage he will have very limited development."

The doctor turned slightly to indicate that he was also speaking for the social worker beside him, and continued, "We recommend that you put David in a state institution where he will receive appropriate care, and try to forget him."

The Blanks were shattered. Only the love of God, mediated through friends, carried them through this crisis and restored a measure of hope. There followed many dark days, but they prayed and reached upward with increasing faith.

After two years of trial and error, in a seemingly miraculous way the opportunity arose to send David to an outstanding school, though it had a long waiting list. The principal even asked to have David enroll.

Now nine years of age, he is able to come home weekends and to play with other children. Someday he will be able to take his place in society, albeit in a humble capacity.

As the Blanks tell their story, not without a trace of tears, there is a glow on their faces. Barbara concludes, "And I have gone back to school to prepare myself to become a teacher of handicapped children."

When this agonizing experience was first thrust on them so unexpectedly, it seemed cruel and impossible to bear. But through the years, prayer, courage, and faith have brought acceptance and peace. And as Barbara prepares herself to teach other Davids, a poignant joy is added to her life and Ralph's.

The Blanks have two other children. The weight and burden of David's handicap could have cast a permanent pall over the family—but it didn't. Because hope and joy were introduced into the situation, a negative, depressed atmosphere was not allowed to take over permanently and stunt the children's emotional growth.

Victorious Christianity is not a matter of enduring pain, but of using it. In a world filled with bad news, the Gospel (good news) stands in stark contrast to the reporting of current events. Hopelessness and despair prevail in international situations, crime waves, amorality, troubled human relationships, and personal problems. In the face of so much anxiety, life has lost its rainbows. Frustration and hopelessness trigger rebellion as an almost automatic response.

Man's great need is not for moralizing, preachments, or even philanthropy. What he needs is personal dignity, achieved in an atmosphere of hope and joy. Jesus often referred to his vision of the Kingdom of God. The Kingdom was to be established in the hearts of men in the immediate present, and fulfilled after death in eternity. This vision gave birth to hope, which so buoyed the hearts of men that they were able to live joyfully through daily toil, suffering, and even persecution.

There is an old folk tale that tells how God summoned the Devil to heaven and complained that he wielded altogether too much power over mankind. He told Satan that he would take away his "tools of the trade." Fearing that he would be stripped of all power, the Devil begged God to leave him one temptation. When God asked what single weapon he chose, Satan said, "Discouragement. For if I can get a man discouraged, it is the wedge that opens the door so that all the other sins known to mankind can come trooping in."

Genuine hope is not escapism, nor is it mere wishful thinking. We do well to face realistically the suffering in the world. Too often Christians have let their religion become an escape from problems, even as suburbia is often an escape from the despair and problems that boil up in the inner city.

But escapism is by no means limited to Christians. Any parent can be surprisingly blind to the loneliness and insecurity of his children. The affluent can all too easily shut their eyes to poverty, or purposely avoid encountering it and alleviating its burden. The white community finds it difficult to comprehend the frustration and anger which is the Negro's heritage after three hundred years of slavery, paternalism, and segregation.

Christianity is not a way out of problems, but a way to meet them. We are not so much "freed from" as "freed for." The Christian walks amid the despair of the world and makes its heartache his own. He walks in the paths of need and loneliness, but he walks in hope, for he keeps step to the rhythm of a distant drummer, and he knows that ultimate victory comes from walking with God.

It is often the task of the Christian to absorb hate and despair, and to transform them into love and hope. Jesus did this on the cross as he received the curses and cruelty of the multitude and prayed for their forgiveness.

Anger and frustration breed a bitter spirit. Communication

is at a standstill when this occurs. Minds are set; dispositions are stubborn; retaliation is the order of the day. There is little disposition to absorb the hate of repressed minorities, or to accept the rebellion of young people as they become nonconformist in dress and manners. Then impasses are formed—physical or spiritual ghettos where we live in separate worlds, non-communicating.

To absorb another's anger, to grant the privilege of catharsis, is to drain off much that prevents fellowship. To surround people with opportunities and hope is to create the climate in which latent potential can begin to be realized.

This is not to say that such an approach is *easy*, but it is *simple*. It is illustrated by the experience of a certain grandfather who was entertaining his son's family at dinner. The three-year-old boy refused to eat his dinner, and when the father insisted, the little fellow threw his plate to the floor in a burst of temper.

The father took the little boy in his arms and started to leave the room, whereupon the child began to pound his father with his fists and yell, "I hate you! I hate you!"

Embarrassed and chagrined, the grandfather could not resist thinking, *I'd never let a child of mine get away with that!* Fortunately, he kept silent.

As the boy screamed and pummelled, the father slowly caressed the lad's head and said, "But I love you. I love you. I love you."

The outburst lasted only a minute or two, and then the child collapsed. The father took him into the next room and rocked him until the sobbing diminished. There followed a quiet talk in which the father spoke of the importance of eating properly. After both of them had washed their faces, they returned to the dining room and the little fellow ate his dinner peacefully. Love had won.

Love requires that we be willing to break old habits and

patterns, abandon the roles that society seems to demand of us, and depart from the "script" that the world has prepared. To do the unexpected, to drop our masks and let go accepted patterns of behavior, is not always easy. In fact, it can be painful and require great courage—but it takes courage to discover the power of love.

The December 1966 issue of "Guideposts" contained a delightful story of a boy playing the part of the Bethlehem innkeeper in the Christmas play at his church. After repeating his line, "I have no room for you. Be gone!" he looked wistfully at the retreating figures of the children playing Joseph and Mary.

They had not gone far down the aisle when the boy's emotions broke through his play acting, and he ran after them crying, "I didn't mean it. I didn't mean it. You don't have to go. Come back. You can have *my* room." The little fellow had rejected the lines of the script and spoken the lines his own heart prompted. His humanity broke through the pattern set for him. Suddenly he became himself.

Habit patterns have a paralyzing effect. A fish was placed in one end of a rather large bowl. A glass partition kept it confined to a small area and it had no alternative but to swim around in a circle. After some weeks the glass partition was removed, but the fish continued to swim around in the same circle, unaware that the restriction had been taken away. There is in all too many of us an inertia that seeks to confine us to the "womb with a picture window." To desire security and protection at the cost of virtually all else is commonplace.

If we as Christians are to learn to love, and not simply seek to be loved, we must dare to abandon the script and let our hearts express themselves freely. Think of the many things Jesus did that he was not "supposed to do": defending the disciples for plucking grain on the Sabbath; talking to a woman in public—and a Samaritan woman, at that; having dinner with Zacchaeus, a tax collector. Jesus broke the accepted patterns and structures of life and was himself.

Because man is made in God's image and God is love, the deepest desire in the heart of man is to love, to care, to be gregarious, to build for brotherhood. Self-preservation has been said to be the law of the jungle, but in fact it is *not* the first law of life. The preservation of the *species* is the law of life, otherwise there would be no "self" to preserve, and to preserve the species requires altruism. We might say therefore that to love others is not only an ideal, but also a practical necessity.

If I am right in asserting that deep down in every human heart is the desire to love, and that its companion drives are caring, understanding, healing broken relationships, protecting and serving those in need, then why are these so rarely manifested in comparison to self-seeking?

There are a host of reasons: prejudices, early-established habits, self-consciousness, resentments and animosities handed down from generation to generation, and many fears—fear of strangers, of the unknown, of being known, of being hurt. These keep the love in us from finding expression. Instead of "loving our enemies," we strike out at them and try to hurt them in an attempt to protect ourselves. How widespread is the fear of the "brush-off"! The adolescent is afraid to ask for a date lest he be turned down. Adults, singly or in groups, are wary of offering friendship lest a rebuff injure their pride.

Jesus had the courage to love. He openly told his friends that he loved them, and urged them to love one another. Yet today even those of us who claim to follow Jesus are loath to declare our love.

A retreat leader who from time to time meets alternately with groups of high school-age youth and their parents has asked these groups if they are in the habit of expressing love for each other. Invariably, less than ten per cent declare that they have ever openly told their families of their affection for them. Sometimes within a given group there is not a single parent who has told his children of his love, nor has the son or daughter openly admitted that he loves his parents.

Various reasons are given to explain this reticence, the most common being that the individuals fear being misunderstood or laughed at. Those within a family theoretically live close together, yet they communicate so little of the basic, positive emotions of life!

Herbert Lindsay was, in general, a conscientious man, but he had fallen into the habit of shutting himself off from his family. He came home from work too tired to be sociable, plunked himself down in an easy chair and buried himself in his newspaper. When his wife asked about his day he answered in monosyllables. He was too exhausted even to play "Monopoly" with his children.

Then Herbert had an encounter with Jesus Christ. This resulted in his facing himself and examining his behavior. He vowed that he would come home buoyant in spirit, ready to enjoy real fellowship with his family. It was not easy to change old habits, of course, and often Herbert would drive around the block several times before coming home, praying for and claiming a willingness to be outgoing.

But it worked. Now he entered the house with a warm kiss for his wife, and time to listen to her and to tell about the day's events. He sat on the floor—not complaining if it was littered with schoolbooks and baseball equipment—and played with his children. Previously his first words on entering the house were such as, "Here, you kids! Pick up your things. This place looks like a pig pen." Now he held his tongue, and before dinner he helped his children to pick up their things, and the task was accomplished quickly and without fuss.

What happened to Herbert Lindsay is that when he gave

up his "right" to quiet and seclusion, he discovered that he *had* no "rights," but only privileges, chief among which was the privilege of loving and serving his family.

He found, further, that his constant fatigue had resulted from a wrong attitude. True, he had been "too exhausted" for recreation with the children, but if they fell to quarreling among themselves he had plenty of energy to bawl them out at the top of his voice. Negative impulses had moved him to action, while positive ones had not.

Now God's spirit of love supplied ample energy for him to be a human being, warm, affectionate, and outgoing. In spite of extreme self-consciousness, Herbert was soon able to put his hand on his son's shoulder and tell him that he was proud of him. This was very difficult for a man who had been taught to hide his emotions, and who had never heard from his own father the words, "I am proud of you." But now as he said it to his own children, he reaped the rewards of a deep and lasting friendship.

In a family where there is much hostility and bitterness, it is not necessarily because the members of that family hate each other. In fact, the reverse may be true. Each one desires to communicate and to love, but there have been misunderstandings, harsh criticisms, over-directiveness, and brush-offs. So love is repressed rather than expressed.

When we fail to express our love, we do so at our own peril, for repressed love turns to resentment and even to something like hatred. We cannot refuse to love one another and at the same time remain unchanged in our personalities. Jesus' command, "Love one another," is in harmony with the basic nature of man. It is therapeutic, providing good mental and physical health as well as a basis for true and lasting communication.

In the play, "Philadelphia, Here I Come," a success both in Britain and on Broadway, one sees the pathetic and heart-breaking attempt of a father and son to break through the silence and habit patterns of years. On the eve of the son's departure from Ireland for America, neither father nor son can sleep. Late at night they go to the kitchen for a snack and are surprised to meet each other there. They fence for positions, search for words, plunge into painful silences. Asides to the audience indicate how hard they are trying to reveal themselves and to be real with each other during these last hours together before their final separation.

Finally the father speaks of a time when they had gone fishing together when the son was ten years old. As if by magic their hearts are suddenly opened through the recollection of this happy incident. The father speaks of baiting the boy's fishhook. The son recalls the experience with joy.

"Oh, how well I remember the ride on the lake in that little red boat!" the son says nostalgically. At last the channel of communication, long closed, is opening.

"No," contradicts the father, " 'twas not a red boat; 'twas a blue one."

And tragedy ensues as each contends for his memory of the insignificant detail to be accepted as correct. Stubbornness on both sides brings back the atmosphere of helpless alienation and the curtain falls on the spectacle of two lonely people unable to remove the barriers that isolate them from each other.

What trivial things hold us apart! Wanting to be right, "edgemanship," preserving personal dignity, defending one's position. Trivial things—but they combine to form a wide gulf between people. We can "win the argument and lose the friend."

The courage to love includes willingness to overcome whatever barriers separate us. Frequently it involves the same quality of laying down our lives that was in Jesus as he laid down his life for us. It involves a brokenness whereby our reputations and pride and status are set aside in order to help us achieve communication.

Alice Fisher was an elderly schoolteacher who lived in retirement on a small piece of property in the country. On the boundary line between Alice's lot and her neighbor's there was an old tree covered with wisteria. The neighbor asked her to have the tree removed, but Alice refused.

One day when she was away, the neighbor cut down her tree, sawed it up for firewood, and put the wood in his own basement. Alice was furious, and nursed her anger for five or six weeks. Then finally the spirit of the Sermon on the Mount entered her heart. She baked a cake and took part of it to her neighbor, only to have the door slammed in her face. Three days later she went back with some cup custards. This time the door was held ajar a few inches, but the gift refused. Alice's next offering was a bouquet of flowers from her garden, and this was accepted with hesitant thanks.

Just a week after this last incident, the neighbor died of a heart attack, and his widow, dazed with grief, turned to Alice for help. During the next dark days the schoolteacher was able to minister to an entire family, and to be a tower of strength to them. How grateful she was that she had given in to God's urging to forget her resentment and to become a peacemaker.

Would to God we spent as much time, energy, and imagination in building friendships as we do in perpetuating feuds! Would to God that modern man knew how to wage peace as well as he knows how to wage war!

God calls us to find the courage to love, to let down our masks, to be willing to be rebuffed, to show our best and deepest selves to our fellowmen. It is the way of hurt and heartache, the way of the cross, but it is the way of healing, for only this quality of love can bring peace to man and to the world in which he lives.

QUESTIONS FOR DISCUSSION

1. How have troubles affected your life? Have these proven to be "blessings"? Name several, if possible.
2. Have you ever had to forgive someone? Make restitution? Did it make a difference in your life subsequently?
3. Think about the important relationships in your life. Do you see God at work in them? What, to you, is a Christlike attitude as applied to interpersonal relationships?
4. What positive steps can you take to improve a bad relationship?

Bob had the gift of doing the unexpected. Everyone in the Youth Fellowship knew that, and looked to him for surprising suggestions. There was an atmosphere of anticipation, therefore, on the Sunday evening when Bob was to lead the Youth Fellowship program.

And he didn't disappoint them. After the opening worship service, he began, "There's not going to be any regular meeting tonight. I'm going to give you one short sentence; then I'll repeat it; then you'll all go into the sanctuary and sit there without saying a word for twenty minutes."

Because the young people liked Bob they were willing to go along with this "program."

"Okay," he said, "here's the sentence: 'Am I for real or am I a phoney?' I'll repeat it: *'Am I for real or am I a phoney?'* Now, scram."

Everyone trooped into the sanctuary and sat down in a pew. For twenty minutes silence reigned. Then Bob called, "Okay. Back to the salt mines!"

When the boys and girls had assembled in a circle, Bob ordered, "Now, give."

For three or four minutes no one "gave." Then Joyce spoke up: "I never thought about it before, but tonight, for the first time, I see that I'm just a great big phoney."

Joyce, of all people! She was the one who spent six or eight hours a week helping the pastor, taking flowers to the sick, running the mimeograph machine, stuffing envelopes. Joyce, the angel of mercy. People even kidded her about sprouting wings.

As if reading their thoughts she went on, "You think I'm such an angel. Well, I'm not. I trample all over my kid brother. He comes home and shows me his drawings and I sneer at them. He tells me a joke and I won't laugh. Then he gets ornery and starts to sass me, and then I *really* go after him. Finally, when he gets to the point where no one can live with him, I leave him for my mother to deal with and I trot off to church to do my little helpful chores."

It was obvious that Joyce had done some real soul-searching and that her confession was sincere. Her voice broke as she concluded, "But I don't really like to be a phoney. From now on I'm going to be different!"

There is power and joy in the single-minded life. People who go off in two or more directions lose their sense of purpose and lack the satisfaction of a unified personality. Often, when someone commits his life to Christ, he will hold back some areas—perhaps not entirely intentionally—to satisfy a selfish spirit. But he will not experience joy in his commitment if it is not total—at least, total insofar as he can see at the moment.

Or sometimes a man will outdo himself in good works or neighborliness or politeness, and then come home and "let down," believing he has a right to a moral holiday. Like Joyce, he compensates for his unusual kindness in one sphere by giving expression to selfish feelings in another. Such a man finds authentic communication impossible. He has an inner phoniness; he lacks the thrust and abandon of the single-minded life.

Ten-year-old Ted was spending the summer on his uncle's farm. It was the first time he had been outside the city for any extended period, and he was fascinated by farm life. In particular he loved two old horses whose work life was over and who had been retired to a back pasture. They were docile animals, and Ted would lead one of them to the rail fence, climb up and onto its back, and ride around the pasture.

Then one day he decided to ride both horses. He had been to the circus and seen the bareback rider who rode with one foot on each of two horses which were harnessed together, and who turned somersaults and performed other tricks from this precarious position.

Accordingly, Ted harnessed the old horses, maneuvered them into a position where he could climb the fence and mount, then timidly took his position with one foot on each broad back.

This accomplished, Ted's courage returned and he bravely called, "Giddap!" All went well for about fifteen feet, but then the horses drew apart and the lad tumbled down between them in a most undignified fashion.

We cannot ride two horses successfully in the arena of life. Jesus said, "You cannot serve two masters. . . . You cannot serve God and money" (Matthew 6:24, NEB). Unless you are a circus performer, you need to ride one horse to know the thrill of a brisk canter. The parallel in daily living is all too clear. Any attempt to pursue two diverse courses leads to disaster. Likewise it is impossible to maintain loyalty to opposing forces.

This is not to say that there is an inherent virtue in single-mindedness, for one can be intensely loyal to and diligent in pursuit of the wrong goals. The man who spends himself in the acquisition of money and property, the woman who zealously strives to maintain a position of power in the community, the young person whose every waking moment is spent in pursuit of sensual enjoyment—all of these demonstrate the power of single-heartedness, but at what cost to themselves and society! No, singleness in itself can be either beneficial or otherwise.

But if one has a high ideal—a worthwhile goal—and devotes himself to it with singleness of purpose: that is a different matter. He himself flourishes, those around him are transformed, and society is enriched.

This is illustrated in the simple and rather homely story of a young girl named Mary. She was president of the Youth Fellowship in her church, and enrolled in the catechism class looking forward to church membership. After the class met for the third time, Mary startled her pastor by saying, "I don't think I can join the church with the others."

"Why not, Mary?" he asked.

"Well," she said slowly, "you have been telling us that to join the church we should be trying to live as Jesus would. In our home we don't live that way."

This was saddening to the pastor, for Mary's father was the church school superintendent and one of the congregation's leaders.

"What do you mean?" he pursued. "What happens at home?"

"Oh, we lose our tempers, shout at each other—sometimes scream. There are lots of tears." Then Mary added in embarrassment, "Of course, it isn't that way all the time."

"Is that the kind of home you want to have when you are married?" the pastor said.

"No, I want my home to different. The kind of home you talk about in class," Mary replied emphatically.

"Then why don't you begin to live that way right now?" he went on.

The girl shrugged her shoulders in resignation. "What can I do? I'm just one."

The pastor pondered for a moment and then said, "How do you go swimming?"

This conversational turn puzzled the girl, and she remained silent as the man went on, "Do you put one toe into the water, and then one toe of the other foot? Do you let the water creep slowly over your feet and ankles while you stand there shivering, hoping that someone else will come and join you?"

Mary answered scornfully, "You know how I go in swimming." The pastor did know, for Mary was the first one in the spring and the last one in the fall to take to the water. No matter what the temperature she plunged straight off the diving board with a beautiful dive. Then the others followed.

"Have you ever thought of living for Christ the way that you go in swimming?"

Mary's forehead wrinkled and her eyes narrowed. Suddenly a light came into her eyes, then a twinkle, and she said lightly, "I'll be seeing you!" and dashed off.

No sooner did she get home than she called, "Mom, may I help you with supper?" Her mother swallowed hard and managed a startled, "Yes!" In a minute the two of them were working together, chatting merrily, but the mother was inwardly dubious. Why was Mary softening her up? What had she done wrong?

During supper, Mary, the oldest of five children, put bibs on the youngest two and helped them to eat. When the meal was over she said to the older two, "What do you say we do the dishes tonight?" Her sparkling tone of voice intrigued them, and in a moment they were happily at work together.

By now both father and mother were raising their eyebrows. "What's her angle? What does she want?" the mother asked. Her husband replied, "I don't know, but it must be something mighty important this time."

Next morning, Mary helped with breakfast and placed a firm kiss on her mother's cheek before she rushed off to catch the school bus. And when the mother stepped into Mary's room, she very nearly needed a heart stimulant! The bed was made, the dresser drawers straightened. When she opened the closet, nothing fell out!

For several days, apparently unaware of her parents' puzzlement, Mary behaved with joyous enthusiasm. Finally they could stand the suspense no longer, and the father said, "Mary, what gives? What have you done, or what do you want to do?"

"There's no angle, Dad," the girl said, tears springing to her eyes. "It's just that I've been talking to the pastor about living with the Spirit of Christ. I thought I'd try it—and these have been the happiest days of my life."

Mary broke down and had a good cry on her father's shoulder. In a few minutes he was acknowledging that he, too, had not been living as he knew he should. In a matter of days a new spirit spread through the entire home. Mary's enthusiasm had been contagious.

Our love takes on a contagious quality when it has a whole-souled abandon. A ballplayer who gives cautiously of his strength, and plays half-heartedly, never sparks the team. It is the abandon, the totality of our commitment to Christ, that sparks others, creates a warm glow, and fans it into a flame.

If we are single-minded and wholehearted about living for Christ, we may communicate best when we are totally unaware of it. Communication suffers when we are concerned about how effective we are, or when we watch for results, hoping that people will listen to us and change their way of life because of our advice or witness. To have part of our mind on what we are saying and part on the effects of our words is to introduce a self-conscious element that is stultifying. But when we pursue a fellowship with abandon, and live with sincerity and self-forgetfulness, God adds an "overplus" far beyond our dreams.

A minister called at the home of a family where the father took little interest in the church and seldom attended services. The minister hoped to persuade the man to join his wife in active membership, and carefully prepared what he had to say.

Sure enough, the following Sunday the man came to church. But imagine the minister's surprise a few weeks later when the man told him, "It wasn't your argument that moved me. But remember how when we were talking little Jimmy came into the room? I was about to send him away when you picked him up, petted him, and played a finger-game with him. I thought to myself, *Any man who loves little children must have something to say from the pulpit.*"

The deepest, most natural acts cannot be faked. They are an unconscious overflow of singleness of heart. The life that glows with assurance and contagious enthusiasm is the life that is totally committed, radiant in its whole-souled purpose. Many a preacher's words lack power because he himself is unsure of his calling and wishes he were in a different situation or perhaps out of the ministry altogether. Perhaps he is preaching about joy and fellowship, but doesn't have it in his own home. Whenever a man's words are not reinforced by the evidence of his life's situation, they lack power and appeal.

Much of our personal interchange is on a level of discussing ideas, methods, and behavior, but does not communicate faith. We teach our children how to pray and instruct them in ethical precepts. But it is entirely possible to learn about Jesus while failing to experience the indwelling Christ. We can learn about God, but not know him as Father and Friend.

Students leave their seminaries full of theological concepts, clinical methods, and psychological techniques. They have studied the Bible long and arduously. But how often does the student exclaim, "It's true! Christ is my Savior. He's alive. I know it. He lives in my heart and in my home!"

One can build a strong institution with techniques and methods, ideas and hard work—but the Church is more than an institution. It is the Body of Christ, where members bear a relationship to him and to one another. This fellowship develops from faith in and commitment to Christ, and leads to the building of his Kingdom and to a resultant unbreakable love for our fellowmen. The act of faith is not transmitted by dissemination of ideas and techniques. It is transmitted as flame passes from torch to torch, by the leap of faith from heart to heart.

Life begets life, and faith kindles faith. We cannot give what we do not possess. And, by the same token, if we have a radiant faith in Christ, if our lives are marked by singleness of heart and we speak and live for the Master with abandon and lack of self-consciousness, we cannot help but communicate faith and make possible the birth of a new spirit in the lives of others.

QUESTIONS FOR DISCUSSION

1. What does it mean to have "both feet on one horse"? What are its advantages?
2. What are you most enthusiastic about? Dedicated to? Committed to?
3. Tell what valuable things have come out of inner conflict in your life. Out of conflict between yourself and others.
4. What is your most important strength or asset?

Johnny Anderson worked in the soft coal mines of Southern Illinois. It was a hard life and a bitter life in the late nineteenth century. For months at a time—from early fall until spring—the mine workers never saw the sun except on Sunday. The company demanded long hours, and Johnny was at the mouth of the pit before sunrise and didn't return home until after dark.

Like most of his fellow workers, Johnny was constantly in debt to the company store. His future was as black as the coal he mined. But he and his wife had a dream: to move north and "homestead" a piece of land.

Then the Government made a large tract of land in northern Wisconsin available to homesteaders and sold it at a dollar an acre to anyone who would take a quarter section or more. Johnny's wife took in extra washing, and by scrimping and saving the Andersons accumulated enough money to buy forty acres of wilderness land.

Johnny took a train to Merrill, Wisconsin, and walked the twenty-five miles to his tract of land in Ormsby. On his back were a sack of flour, an axe, and a few other essentials. It was July, the season of mosquitoes, horse flies, and "no see'ems," insects whose bite burned like fire. In the closed-in woods it was unbelievably hot and muggy.

As Johnny set about felling trees, he dreamed of the log cabin he would build, and of freedom from the black dust and semi-slavery of the coal mines. He was a strong man, and tough. He had brought no gloves, believing that the calluses built up by using pick and shovel in the mines would protect his hands. But the work was different, the axe handle wore away at unexpected places, and in a short time his hands were raw and bleeding. Insects plagued him and his temper grew short.

The second day was almost unbearable. Johnny gave vent to his pain and frustration, and the woods rang with the sound of his curses as well as the chop, chop of his axe.

When the third day dawned, Johnny was an exhausted man. His spirit and energies were at their lowest. He shouted out curses with greater violence, and the very emptiness of the woods seemed to mock him. There was not even an audience for his oaths!

Finally he could take it no longer. The insects, the heat, and the bleeding hands had won. He slumped to the ground cursing God and man with all the vehemence remaining to him. He cursed himself that he had ever dreamed of a log cabin in the northern woods. His shoulders shook and great sobs racked his body.

After some time he stopped crying and there came a moment of strange stillness. Suddenly, mingled with the whir of insects and the quiet forest noises, there was a new sound. Johnny listened intently, straining his senses to hear. Though it came from miles away, there could be no mistake: it was the ring of an axe. Another homesteader was felling trees. Somewhere, another man was dreaming a dream; another father was providing for his family. Somewhere, in spite of insects, bleeding hands, and bone weariness, another man was clearing land and building for the future.

Slowly Johnny straightened up, spat on his raw hands,

grabbed his axe, and went to work. Years later he sat in the log cabin that he had built, and in which he had raised a fine family, and told a spellbound guest this story of how the ring of another man's axe had given him courage to go on when discouragement had nearly defeated him.

Man is created with twin needs, for solitude and fellowship. There are times when we must walk through life's turnstiles one by one, each alone. There are decisions that each man must make for himself, and he neglects to make them at his own peril, for something dies in us when we refuse to face life and take action. Yet we stand constantly in need of our fellowmen, for we cannot live fully unless we live in community.

Johnny Anderson would have found little joy in a log cabin built by another and handed to him. He alone had to match his strength with life. He alone had to wrestle with and even defy God. He alone needed to test his powers and prove his purposes.

Yet he also needed his fellowmen. The cocky individualist had to be broken, and in his brokenness to hear the word of God spoken by the ringing axe of a fellow human being.

Paul caught this paradox in two sentences placed only three verses apart in his letter to the Galatians: "Bear one another's burdens," and "Each man will have to bear his own load (6:25)." Man must both stand on his own feet and live in loving interdependence with others.

The creation of man in God's image as a unique individual, possessed of free choice, sets him apart as one who wants to engage in reflection, creative thinking, consideration of values, the choice of goals toward which he will bend his efforts. By the same token, all other men are created in God's image, and therefore from the same matrix. No man is an island, for each is a distinct part of the mainland. In maturity, man becomes more and more deeply aware of belonging to his brothers.

Deep in the soul of the individual is that which desires to stand alone, to win the race, to rebel against the status quo, to espouse some great cause. It is natural for man to seek to maintain his integrity by taking a solitary position. The late Sam Shoemaker used to say that a man does not truly know and lean upon God unless he has come to the place where he can say, "God and the Christ-way of life mean so much to me that if every other person in the world denied and forsook him, I would still believe in him and maintain this way of life."

Here the soul reaches up in solitary grandeur like an Alpine peak in the morning sun. Such a soul stood revealed in Martin Luther when he faced his accusers and said, "Here I stand. God help me, I can do no other." The strength for such a stand derives from personal aloneness with God. A man can cultivate the habit of frequent encounters with the eternal God through thought and prayer, through communion with nature and art, through solitary decisions. But then, if he is to be a whole man, he must translate his decisions and convictions into confrontation, encounter, and communication with his fellowmen.

Solitude is given to us in order that we may reflect on life, encounter the Spirit of God as we know him in Jesus Christ, discover his will for us, and come to decisions about the direction our lives should take. Here the "I" within me stands revealed. I see myself in the pages of the Bible—both the self I am and the self I can become. As I reflect on the passing drama of life, something in me says, "I belong here; I am part of all this." I am judged, laid bare, rebuked, healed, restored, and sent forth.

Yet Paul Tillich reminds us that aloneness can deteriorate into self-pity as well as reach the majesty of solitude. When it becomes an occasion for self-centered despair. solitude has been perverted and has lost its power to be an integrating factor in life. Self-pity is a damning, destructive force to the human soul.

However, there is a kind of despair that solitude *should* include. Albert Camus takes us Christians to task for passing too lightly over the miseries of the world, and he is right. Hiroshima, Dachau, the sidewalks of Calcutta, and the ghettos in the heart of America's cities are all realities. In solitude we should not only come to grips with needs of our own hearts, but with the suffering and sin of the world. And, obviously, it is not enough merely to think about them: solitude should prepare us to do battle with them.

In aloneness we also come to know the triumphs of our Master and the miracle of change in us that can make for our triumph. Out of Jesus' solitary struggle in Gethsemane came great victory. Gethsemanes are always endured alone; the angels do not come to minister to us until we have wrestled with a problem and made a decision.

No one can decide for us. God honors the freedom of choice he has given us, and he will not stoop to coercion. Each of us, in his aloneness, must decide for right or wrong, for Christ or for self, and whether he will do something to rid the world of the monsters that stride through it—war, poverty, racism, corruption, graft—or stand by as a spectator. Man violates his integrity if he does not think his own thoughts and come to his own decisions. The Christian must go beyond this, and attempt to think *God's* thoughts, sense *his* burdens, and build *his* Kingdom.

But if solitude is essential, fellowship is no less so. From earliest times man has lived in families and tribes. He is by nature gregarious, and when he partakes of a new nature in Christ his gregarious instinct is heightened in the rich and wonderful fellowship (koinonia) which Christ gives to his people. Man is made for brotherhood; he is made to love his fellows, to work with them, to know and be known by them.

One's particular community may be his family, his fellow workers, his fishing cronies, his coffee-break friends, his fellow churchmen. As a social being, he needs to be in communication, whether with his wife or his golfing partner. In silence he has thought and received; in fellowship he speaks and acts. Within the group the individual's ideas are hammered and tested on the anvil of argument, dialogue, and criticism. Within the group he seeks to spell out and objectify the dreams that have come to him in solitude.

But acts tend to fall far short of dreams. If in solitude I resolve to love, I may not be able in real life to enact that love. Nevertheless, it is in action that we make thought an integral part of our being. It is transferred from mind to muscle.

There is a give and take in fellowship, whether at the family breakfast table, in the prayer group, at the office, or in the community, that lays bare the irrationalities of our thoughts and plans that seemed so logical in solitude. As we learn to listen deeply to our fellowmen and live with the hearts and minds of others, we are stripped of our sentimentality, jealousy, and competitiveness, and we see our ideas in a new light. It is often a mark of a man's strength that he is able to change his way of thinking and alter his action in the light of God's wisdom which comes to him through fellowship with others.

Both solitude and fellowship may seem threatening. There is a strange ambivalence in man, for though he needs both aloneness and interaction, each one holds certain fears for him and may create anxiety within him. Here is Leonard, for example, who would like to get along well with people yet dreads to be known. He is afraid of being judged, of being hurt. He escapes into solitude, work, and self-pity. He hides in his room, reading books and watching television.

And here, by contrast, is Elizabeth. The very thought of being alone for more than a few minutes at a time fills her with dread. She cannot face herself, or make decisions, and therefore she engages in a whirl of activity, working on committees, wasting time in endless small talk, playing bridge, wandering through the supermarket on unnecessary shopping trips. At the end of the day Elizabeth is physically exhausted and falls asleep almost as soon as her head hits the pillow. She will not think about problems; she will not be introspective; she has no desire to encounter reality.

This is the existence of those who are only half-men, shunning the crowd on one hand and aloneness on the other. The Holy Spirit is saying to some of us, "Spend more time alone," and to others, "Get into depth and honest action with people." Dietrich Bonhoeffer asserts that a man cannot truly enter into community with others unless he knows how to live in solitude. Likewise, he cannot truly live in solitude unless he has deeply encountered the lives of others.

Anne was a woman who lost her husband in World War II. Five years later she remarried. Only a year after that her second husband, Walter, was killed during army maneuvers. Anne retreated to her home, where she sat alone with the doors and windows closed, bereft of hope and courage. Visitors were subjected to an endless barrage of self-pity: "Why did God do this to me? There is no justice. Both of my husbands killed in the service! Why did it have to be my Walter?"

For seven or eight weeks Anne's pastor visited her almost daily, trying to give comfort and to absorb her self-pity and grief and to lead her back to normalcy. Nothing the pastor did or said had any effect on Anne. At last, in desperation, he told her that she would never find victory as long as she kept asking "Why?" Taking down the old family Bible from the shelf, he turned to the Gethsemane passage and asked Anne to read it aloud: "Father, if it be possible let this cup pass from me; neverthelesss, not my will but thine be done."

The pastor said, "God did not want Jesus' death any more than you wanted Walter's death. But untimely death comes in a world of hate. Will you accept it even as Jesus did? Will you give your husband over into God's keeping? Do it now, audibly."

Anne wept and shook her head, but in a few minutes she haltingly spoke the words her pastor had suggested. When her prayer was completed, a look of peace came over her face. She was a different person.

What's more, within a few days she had established new relationships with her family and neighbors. Because she had first come to terms with herself and with God, she was able to enter the community once again.

If a person seeks to enter into community without first partaking of solitude, he brings little or nothing of value to the group. He is likely to be a sponge or a leaner. But if he has been faithful in his tryst with God, he comes to the fellowship with strength. He does not become a parasite, but a contributor and a participant in the interplay of ideas and experiences. Fellowship takes on a creative dimension for him. When one shares his thoughts and experiences, he strikes sparks within the spirits of others, and the entire group can come into an amazing awareness of new truth.

On the other hand, if one seeks solitude who has not cultivated fellowship with others, he does not bring to his aloneness the cries and hopes of his fellowmen. He does not know the agonies of the world. His ideas have not been tested in community. He tends to seek escape, to avoid encounter and involvement, even to enjoy the ecstasies of fantasy—or the perverse pleasure of self-pity. How easy it is to fabricate an ideal world if we refuse to enter the real world and live out the mandates of Christ in concrete situations.

The whole man is at home in both solitude and fellowship. When he says, "Enter, God," his aloneness takes on a nobler character. Like his Master, he is at ease in silence. He knows the vigil of prayer, communion with God, and the wrestlings with self-will. But, also like his Master, he moves into fellowship. He lives in honest encounter with his friends. He opens his heart in deep love to other men, risking rejection and ridicule. He performs the humblest services, demands the most difficult behavior from himself, espouses causes on behalf of the oppressed. He is often unpopular, but he is found wherever the battle is fiercest and the burden heaviest.

The fellowship of those who have known God in solitude is the coming together of men who are strong in the Lord. Their strength is then multiplied, for the Holy Spirit works with great power among men who know the Risen Lord and who meet "in one accord."

QUESTIONS FOR DISCUSSION

1. What tends to make people escape into solitude? Lose themselves in a crowd? Have you experienced either or both of these things?
2. When have you most benefited from being alone? Being in fellowship?
3. Where do you now need most to grow—in solitude? In relationships?

Is your marriage a bit of heaven—or a bit of hell on earth? Are marriage problems taking the joy out of life? Marriage is the most intimate of human relationships and a married couple can draw the worst from each other as well as the best. There *are* ways to deal with marital problems—ways which have been discovered by countless husbands and wives who have looked to Jesus Christ for answers. Jesus came to show us the gateway to heaven on earth.

In a marriage which has come into rough waters, it is possible for one of the partners to get the ship back on an even keel if he is willing to begin with himself.

Forget the old American game of passing the buck. Resist the impulse to say, "Our marriage would be so much better if my wife (husband) would only change!" The one who seeks Christ's answer to his dilemma should recall that he said, "Follow *thou* me."

Broken marriages begin to mend and communication is reestablished when one of the partners is willing to make a breakthrough and say, "Lord, begin with me. I am the one who needs to change, to love more deeply and more wisely." Even if you think your spouse is one hundred per cent wrong, when you stand in the presence of Christ you will begin to see that you, too, have shortcomings. You will discern where you have failed to accept responsibility for the marital relationship, and you will be able to say, "God, change me." The Christian is committed to follow Christ who went all the way in love, all the time. So, for a start, stop demanding that your partner change his ways. Let God start changing *you.*

Forgive, and forget the past. Dwelling on past hurts, bringing up past faults, or limiting one's present acts by expecting a repetition of past behavior only builds up emotional barriers. How easy it is to "imprison" your partner mentally in a certain pattern of behavior, thereby condemning him to remain unchanged. Our faith is in a God who can and does work miracles, both in ourselves and in others.

In prayer, forgive your spouse for whatever has happened. Go even further and accept responsibility for all the misunderstandings that have grown up between the two of you. Needless to say, your partner cannot receive your forgiveness unless he repents. God forgives you, even before you sin, so practice forgiveness toward your spouse regardless of attitudes you may feel justified in expecting from him.

If past experiences distress you, if negative memories haunt you so that the flow of God's love through you to your partner or your children is hindered, first talk these things over with God in deep and honest prayer, claiming victory. If this does not bring emotional release, then talk through these experiences with a trusted Christian friend. Pray with him for forgiveness.

In the event that past situations still dam up the flow of your love, it may help to recreate and relive those experiences vividly in your imagination, one at a time, talking them out with your friend. Let Christ enter each incident as you relive it, giving you victory in it then and there.

One night Barney MacDonald came home drunk and cursing his wife, Miriam. It was the first time such a thing had happened. The memory of this incident returned again and again to haunt and frighten her. Years passed, but still she often dwelt on this experience in her mind.

One day Miriam recounted the scene in detail to a Christian friend. She told of running from her husband that night, locking herself in her bedroom, and bursting into tears.

The friend said, "Here and now, recreate that scene in your imagination, but instead of running from Barney, go toward him as he slumps in his chair. Lay your hands on his head and pray for him aloud. Pray for God's love to enter into his whole being."

When Miriam had done this, her friend went on: "Now, in your mind's eye, take off your husband's shoes, make him comfortable on the couch, prepare some coffee for him. Then sit down quietly and wait with him while he sleeps."

In a little while the wife reported that this was done. Suddenly she said, "I've just remembered that before Barney went out that evening we had some words. I blurted out some of my own ideas and squelched his. I had forgotten that completely."

Later she recounted this entire incident to her husband, including her acceptance of personal responsibility for his drinking and angry words. The dark memory was banished and the young couple came to a new understanding of each other. How imperative it is to clean the slate, to receive God's forgiveness, to forgive one's mate and one's self, and to claim victory over anything in the past that may "drag anchor" in a relationship!

One cannot love and relate warmly to other people until he has accepted them as they are, faults and all. Happiness can begin with a realistic acceptance of one's partner, children, and life situation. Misery and frustration result from living in "If-Only-Land." ("If only Jack spent more time at home!" "If only Helen would pay attention to how she looks!" "If only our daughter behaved herself!" "If only we lived in a better neighborhood!")

Living in such a dream world, we tend to see our partners as they might be: more successful financially, more attractive, better able to cope with social situations. As we continue to think of how our spouse might be, we set up a fantasy image of a different kind of mate that could be ours if only the present one would change! This dream picture becomes the object of our affections. Slowly we fall in love with the fantasy and out of love with the real thing. Small wonder that we become irritated with our partner, since he does not measure up to our fantasies.

God loves us as we are. He does not say, "If only you would clean yourself up a little, I would love you." Paul wrote, "God shows His love for us in that while we were yet sinners Christ died for us" (Romans 5:8). He accepts us as sinners. He knows that we will always slip and fall, yet he is committed to loving us just as we are, and he will continue this love toward us through countless failures. To love others with God's kind of love is to love them without conditions.

A wife who was left alone evening after evening started to keep a "hate book," making careful note of the time her husband was not at home. She wrote down the exact number of minutes he was with her during his waking hours. He spent only two evenings at home in seven weeks, most often dining out with business associates. His wife recorded it all, waiting for an appropriate time to face him with the devastating statistics.

Meanwhile, God began to work in her heart. He showed her that she was so bitter that the few minutes she did have with her husband were made doubly unhappy. The thought came to her: "Why not make those moments together interesting and pleasant?" So the hate book was thrown into the fire and the brief intervals with her husband were packed full of love and laughter.

Within weeks he began to spend more time at home, and soon afterwards he faced up to the way he had been short-changing his family. Foundations were laid for a new and more satisfying relationship in the home.

Much of our behavior is conditioned by the way others act toward us. If someone is grumpy and complaining, we tend to react negatively. We also tend to reflect pleasant, outgoing attitudes. Thus we are often reflectors rather than initiators.

When Christ makes us "new creatures" in marriage, we are freed from the tyranny of reaction to environment. It is not his will that we be conditioned by the moods of others, but rather that his Spirit flow through us in such a way that we *act* in accordance with His love.

This is the positive attitude. The secret of acceptance which is not abject lies in thanking and praising God for people as they are and for situations as they exist. See the good in people; see the hand of God in life situations. Pray such prayers as: "Thank you, God, for this partner of mine. Help me to be aware of the good in him, and concentrate on that." The psalmist's words, "Magnify the Lord with me," can be paraphrased as, "Magnify the good (the God) in my partner with me."

When reverses come, we can ask, "God, what are you trying to tell me through this?" whether the "this" be an illness, an accident, or a flat tire. Acceptance is the prelude to relaxation and the ability to sense God's leading more clearly in any given situation.

Frequently a husband or wife will try to make over his partner by obvious or subtle means. He plays God by trying to change his spouse to fit some preconceived pattern. Though the change may be a much-needed one, there is a built-in resistance in every human being against any attempt to change him. Outside pressure sets up inner resistance.

Conversely, setting a man free and surrounding him with an atmosphere of release and joyous naturalness throws him upon his own inner resources. Surrounding him with love provides a pathway over which God's Spirit may come into his life. The promptings of the Spirit reach deep, and ultimately man heeds them and obeys from inner desire rather than from outward constraint.

To set people free, to love them as they are, is to place them in the stream of God's Spirit, so that His love and power may go to work. Few married people can answer the question, "Have I set my partner completely free?" with an unqualified *Yes*.

Yet God's love, the norm for Christians, is not possessive. The parable of the Prodigal reminds us again that the father sets his son free even to go into the far country and to live in sin. No matter how far the son wanders, his father's love follows. Such freedom does not condone sin, but it does give opportunity for life's experiences to teach valuable lessons.

God honors our personhood by granting us freedom of choice, freedom to obey or disobey him. Jesus set Peter free, even to deny him. We ought also to honor the personhood of our mates by setting them free to be themselves. However, to set others free does *not* mean to divorce ourselves from their lives. It does *not* mean to withhold information that might be of value to them. If we see someone driving toward a washed-out bridge, we are obliged to warn him to stop!

Setting someone free to be himself should also free us from hidden motives. It is easy to love a partner so that he may be more loving in return, more attentive and more responsive to our needs. It is easy to train children so that they will be good, less trouble to us, and more flattering to our egos. Thus we see that we often love with an ulterior motive, hoping to get something in return.

Love with an "angle" is not ideal. It is not God's kind of love. God loves for the sheer joy of loving because he *is* love. When God's love is in a man's heart, he loves others in this way—or at least approaches this ideal. It makes love possible under difficult circumstances, when mistakes have been made and when the situation is disastrous, humanly speaking.

Fellowship within marriage includes many things which might be summed up in the word *encounter*. A meaningful encounter involves both speaking and listening. Paul wrote of "speaking the truth in love" (Ephesians 4:15), which we may take to mean a willingness to be honest and transparent with others and so to listen that we sincerely seek to understand them, appreciate them, and share in their interests.

Our aim in marriage should be to be increasingly known to each other through the years. The process is never completed: first because man is growing and changing day by day and thus there is always something new about him, and second because he is made in God's image and therefore there is a depth and a mystery about him that is never completely penetrable by another or even by himself.

Honesty is part of love. A couple should be able to be honest about their thoughts, fears, deeds, motives, and desires. To live behind a mask is to deny one's partner the privilege of knowing his inner self. It also robs one of the power of a single-minded life.

For fifteen years of marriage a certain man had been living behind a facade of graciousness, chivalry, and kind deeds. His wife loved this wonderful image of her husband, thinking it to be the real man. Then one day, because of the torment in his heart, he unburdened himself to his wife: his deep anxieties, fear, loneliness, cowardice, pride, lust, and strong desire for praise and for people's approval.

The wife had no idea that such confusion and conflict lay beneath her husband's placid exterior. For the first time, she really knew him, and the "real he" felt known and loved at last. Because his wife had entered deeply into his heart, he was set free from living behind a pretense. The marriage was made new and there was a sudden sense of the reality of God's presence in both man and wife. Subsequently, they found new openness to other people, and freedom to love and to be loved by them.

When we lack the courage or willingness to be known, the process of speaking the truth in love can be short-circuited. For example: Fred is late again for dinner and Norma, furious because her carefully-prepared meal is ruined, is impulsively sarcastic. Throughout the meal they sit in silence. Fred feels guilty, but his pride won't allow him to say, "I'm sorry." Instead, he goes to the kitchen with Norma and helps her with the dishes, or puts up those hooks in the closet that she's been asking him to attend to for weeks, or, if he has to go out again that evening, he comes home with candy or flowers. Another substitute for honest apology may be to make love to his wife.

All of these—helping with household chores, gifts, sexual overtures—are suspect, for they have the ulterior motive of seeking to reestablish communication without the pain and humbling of a forthright apology.

But suppose that during dinner Fred admits his fault and says, "I'm sorry, Dear. I could have phoned when I knew I was going to be late."

Norma is likely to respond with, "There was no need for me to be so nasty." Relief comes, and a smile or a kiss seals the friendship anew. Now Fred's help, or gift, or sexual attention is quite different: not the means to an end, but the overflowing of a relationship already established. The ordinary things of life therefore take on a sacramental nature.

Many people never realize how difficult it is for their marriage partners to reveal their inmost feelings and hidden needs. Often one mate will be gregarious, impulsive; the other reticent and inhibited. It is costly for the latter to be honest, and his spouse may not sense this fully. The quick pronouncements and glibness of one may threaten the other.

Wise is the spouse who learns how to listen so as to make it easier for his mate to speak. The corollary of speaking the truth in love is hearing it. This may rule out quick rejoinders, and involve receiving one's partner's words in silence, with a caress, or with a meaningful but unspecific statement such as, "The more I know you, the more I love you."

If *speaking* and *hearing* the truth in love are essential to each other, even more so are *giving* and *receiving* love. In fact, all of these processes are inextricably intertwined.

Experience convinces me that a man needs *supportive* love, while a woman needs *tenderness* and *assurance*. It is all too common for a woman to compete with and undercut her husband, and for him to take her for granted. Again and again this unhappy scene is played out: the husband returns home after a difficult day to be greeted with complaints and resentment. He flops into an armchair and hides behind a newspaper.

The wife will do well to remember that, no matter how tedious her day may have been, her husband needs to be built up and undergirded with love and faith. And the husband should appreciate his wife's longing for contemporary fellowship after being confined to children and household concerns all day.

She needs assurance, tenderness, and the expression of affection—apart from and in addition to sexual intercourse—and she may bid for these, subtly or with questions such as: "Why don't you tell me anymore that you love me?" The worst possible rejoinder to such bids for affection is a glib remark: "I married you, didn't I?"

It seems that men, more than women, are afraid to express their love. They may feel that it isn't "manly," or they may actually fear rejection. Instead of forgiving, trying again, being willing to be hurt, they withdraw into a shell, become gruff, or assume an air of surprised innocence.

The ploys women use are equally devious. But just as one partner may initiate a quarrel or create an uncomfortable atmosphere, so either one may reverse the process.

Love always costs, and sometimes it costs in pain. Christians see the truth of this in the Cross. Jesus frequently got the brush-off, but He was neither afraid nor ashamed to love, to tell his friends that he loved them, even though his love might be rejected.

Where there is love in marriage, there is always the possibility of a fresh start. This requires frank encounter, a talking-over of problems, a willingness to discuss and to see the other partner's point of view.

However, bear in mind that there is a right time and a wrong time to initiate such encounter situations. The time to raise the question of tangled finances is *not* when Sam comes home tired and cross from a hard day at the office. The time to plan Grandmother's visit is *not* when Doris has been up all night with a sick child. Dialogue, especially that which involves sensitive areas, should be kept away from the time of crisis or emotional upset.

Problems frequently arise in marriage when there is conflict over dividing areas of responsibility. Even when a couple agrees at the outset to divide up tasks in a certain way, changing circumstances and unforeseen situations can cause the arrangement to become impractical, and relations between husband and wife may deteriorate unless steps are taken to readjust.

Nowhere are such conflicts more obvious than in questions of finance. Let us look at three possible approaches to this one area, which suggest parallels in other aspects of married life.

Money questions can be dealt with in three general ways: fifty-fifty (an eye for an eye); separate domains; and joint decisions under God.

The first of these is highly competitive and immature. "You spent seventy-five dollars for golf clubs, so I can spend seventy-five dollars for a new dress." "You got a new vacuum cleaner; I'm going to get a new car radio." Husband and wife compete for "their share" of the family income, and enjoying things together becomes increasingly difficult. The negative aspects of the arrangement add their own irritants: "If we can't send Junior to camp, then we can't afford that power lawn mower."

It is possible that this jockeying for position may be accomplished with good humor, especially in the event that there is an adequate income, but in the long run it accomplishes no common purpose, and it can lead to a constant battle of wits and sometimes emotions.

In the second case, couples decide to take separate areas of responsibility (separate domains). The husband is responsible for house and car payments, insurance, major appliances, tuition, and savings; the wife handles household expenses, luxury items, vacations, and charities.

This arrangement can be beneficial when arrived at by mutual consent, especially if unusual or major decisions are talked over together. However, separate areas of responsibility are sometimes dictated by a dominant partner, in which case trouble can result. For example, if the husband asserts himself unnecessarily and establishes "the rules," his wife may be unhappy because she has little or nothing to say about important questions—whether to buy a new car, whether to set aside a college fund, whether to help provide for aging parents.

Or if the wife is the dominant partner, the husband may become less and less confident as the years go by. His preferences may be by-passed, and as time passes the process of arriving at mutual decisions becomes more difficult.

Often it is the line of least resistance for one partner to take charge and make decisions. A man may not trust his wife to handle money, and rather than take the time and energy to help her grow in this area, he asserts himself more and more forcibly. Conversely, he may abdicate his responsibility simply to avoid conflicts.

In such unhappy situations, the couple avoids the encounter of coming to know why one differs widely from the other. Often, tendencies to prodigality or miserliness go back to childhood privation or fear which may still control current behavior. It takes much painful opening of heart and much patient listening to work through these differences. It calls for honest confrontation, but the couple in need of this step should not hold back because of the fear of being hurt or the dread of the pain of inner growth.

Countless decisions throughout the day are private decisions made with the loved one in mind: the wife chooses her husband's favorite fish for dinner; the husband picks up a couple of tickets to a movie his wife wants to see. But when the decisions involve issues where there is a marked divergence of opinion—here is the place for patient, understanding, *joint* decisions, made openly, lovingly, and sometimes at the cost of one of the two "giving in."

By far the most productive and ideal method of dealing with decisions is to make them together under God. This rules out the possibility of taking over areas of responsibility in open defiance, in secret, by emotional blackmail, or by constantly placating the offended partner.

The prelude to making joint decisions under God is the commitment of the partners to him, as individuals and as a team. It relies on wisdom and direction greater than that of either partner, claimed by faith. Practically, it means examining all the factors involved, "putting the cards on the table," including pertinent data, inner motives and desires, the recognition of which spouse has greater experience in the particular area, and lessons learned in the past.

To find God's will in a situation where there is a serious difference of opinion between husband and wife, let each partner be willing to relinquish his own desire and set aside his own point of view, and be open to follow any possible plan, whether it comes from his spouse or from an outside source. By experience we find that God's will is not necessarily the husband's or the wife's, but an entirely different way. When followed, it brings a deep sense of rightness.

Couples who believe in God and who are committed to him, and who have learned how to release their own desires even in sensitive areas, have discovered countless times that if they will silently and prayerfully "listen," each asking God to reveal his plan, *the same thoughts* will occur to both partners. These may be taken as God's leading until such time as a strong inner contrary leading comes.

To be able to talk together without raised voices and without bullying, nagging, hurt feelings, self-pity, or self-righteousness, is a sign of growing maturity. The desire to be right should always be subordinated to the desire to see and understand the other's point of view. The question is not, "Who's right?" but "What's right?"

Few people are so difficult to live with as those who are "always right," especially if they insist on letting others know how right they are. Almost as difficult are those who behave like doormats and claim the alibi of always being wrong, accepting the blame, and thus avoiding honest encounter. True fellowship sparks new ideas, draws out hidden potential, creates new dreams, and sets the stage for real growth in marriage. Such encounter should always occur in deep love. More and more this brings out what is womanly in woman and manly in man.

When differences in points of view persist, and the situation arises where one partner firmly insists on his way, the other may hasten the process of mutual understanding and eventual agreement by simply giving in, accepting in love the other's leading, and going along with it gracefully. If the decision should prove right, let the partner who has given up his way be quick to acknowledge its rightness. Should it prove wrong, let him not gloat, be self-righteous, or seek to press his advantage, but rather wait in good humor, believing that God's Spirit will eventually prompt the insistent one to see his mistake.

Doing things together—whether camping, praying, bowling, papering the living room, or working in a settlement house—can be exciting and rewarding when entered into with mutual enthusiasm. There is a time for talk and confrontation; there is also a time to forget differences and unresolved problems and engage in common activities. It may be music, books, or baseball. Picketing as well as prayer draws people together.

When a couple faces sickness, financial privation, community needs, or church tasks, there can be a deepening unity. Not only the family that "prays together" but also the family that plays together and works together "stays together." All shared experiences make a common bond, provided that we engage in them with wholeness of heart.

A man and woman who have conscientiously sought the answer to a problem over a period of time, without results, conceivably might do well to put the problem on the shelf, "take a breather," and do something entirely different together just for sheer merriment. A change of perspective can result from a change of pace or scene.

Often problems that are completely outside the home are solved in the relationship of husband and wife within the home. It made a big difference, for example, to the fifty men who worked under a certain foreman's direction when his wife decided to get up and give him a good breakfast, a smile, and a kiss. Instead of going to work sourly after a makeshift breakfast alone, he went with a light step and a song in his heart, and fifty men reaped the benefits.

A wife who felt neglected and unloved, and whose teaching ability was ignored while she wallowed in self-pity, was given a new lease on life when her husband saw his selfishness and began to treat her with tenderness and consideration. Released from the burden of neglect, she felt a new desire to be of use in her community, and a number of slum children who needed tutoring benefited from her time and ability as a teacher.

Examples like these raise the larger question: to what purpose is improved communication between husband and wife? To save a marriage? To benefit the children? To make the home more pleasant? These are starting points, not goals. It is a spiritual law that we can only keep what we give away. To hold on to a loving relationship is to lose it.

The end purpose of Jesus' life was not to build a warm relationship with his disciples, but to build the Kingdom of God. You and I are likewise called to build the new world, the reign of the Spirit of Christ on earth. A transformed home is not an end in itself, but a miniature of the Kingdom: the new world under Christ in microcosm.

From out of the love and fellowship of such a home, a man goes each day to his work to live out in the larger context what he has discovered with his wife and family. The wife, too, moves in her sphere of activity at home and in the community as one who is secure and radiant, sure of the love of God, of her husband, and of her children.

For them, the home is a center of love and growth, of confrontation and discipline, of understanding and trust, and a bulwark of power and support. From a home of this kind, the various members go out strengthened to live a new quality of life in Christ that communicates itself in widening circles.

A retired couple rejected the prospect of shuffleboard in Florida, and today they travel over the country telling of a joyous and more vital way of life. A young couple, having found in Christ the answer to their personal needs, have introduced scores of men and women to study and depth groups in their church, and to personal dedication to Christ. A doctor and his wife are finding new motivation in Christ, and a new desire to be teammates, and they now spend three months each year practicing medicine and nursing in an undeveloped part of Africa.

Verbal acknowledgment of God's presence in the home greatly intensifies the love and closeness of a husband and wife. Most married people remember the first time they said "I love you" to each other. The verbal declaration caused their love to leap ahead, the affirmation strengthening the bond that already existed. Love blooms when it is sincerely verbalized.

In the same way, many husbands and wives have thought, "Dear God, I love her," or "Thank you, God, for Jim." God leans over the parapet of heaven, urging us to say it aloud. To express our love and gratitude for each other in audible prayer is to affirm what is already present, and it sets the stage for new growth. Do not hesitate to pray out loud because you want to compose a "nice" prayer. Let the sincere and honest sentence burst through: "God, I sure love my wife! Thank you for her. Make me the husband I ought to be."

Any plan for family prayer should be suited to the needs of the various members; the family should not be suited to a plan. A workable pattern for family prayers is likely to evolve if questions like these are asked: "In what way can husband and wife express their gratitude to God in the presence of their children? In what way can the Bible come alive to the various members of the family? How can we learn to pray simply and sincerely, without embarrassment?"

There should also be a time of prayer for husband and wife alone, when hearts are bared and honesty and love prevail, and when opportunity is given for apology and forgiveness. Some couples make a habit of sitting down together to work on family finances, spreading out the bills on the table, audibly thanking God for his providence and asking for his guidance in the stewardship of his gift to them. Others will take advantage of a trip, long or short, to pray together, to commit the journey to God who has promised to bless our "goings out and comings in." Or in the peace and relaxation that follows sexual intercourse, a couple may whisper a prayer of thanks for each other.

QUESTIONS FOR DISCUSSION

1. Why is it important to combine honesty with love? What is honesty without love? Love without honesty?
2. Is it possible to love unlovely people? How do you do it?
3. Do you believe love can be rekindled? Have you found ways to achieve this? What are they?
4. Who loved you when you most needed it? When you were most unlovely? How did he do it?

Frank Sloan was only five years old, but he was already an expert at driving people crazy.

In his first year at nursery school, he "went through" four teachers. Now, in his second year, the school's principal had taken Frank into her own class—but she, too, was at her wit's end. One evening she was entertaining out-of-town friends at dinner and unburdening herself to them.

"I've used every technique I know. I've been patient; I've given him more time and attention than the other pupils; I've run the gamut of disciplinary measures—and all to no avail. Frank throws his work on the floor, knocks his crackers and milk off the table, slaps and even bites the other children. It doesn't seem fair to allow him to be in the school and disrupt our entire program. What would you do in my place?"

Her guests considered the problem for a moment, and then one of them said, "Nancy, you're the most gifted teacher I know. Moreover, you are a dedicated Christian. On the face of it, there's not much to suggest.

"But," he went on, "God must have a plan for Frank. The child probably has sixty or seventy more years to live. What happens to him now is very important. Why don't we be silent for a while and see what thoughts God puts into our minds about what is to be done."

For five minutes or so, Nancy and her guests were quiet. Finally the school principal broke the silence. "I don't like to say what came to me, but here it is. God said, 'You really don't love Frank. It makes you happy to greet the children each morning until Frank comes along. Then you tighten up and pray for patience. He has became a burdensome problem to you. If he is absent, you are relieved. The fact is that you feel you are on the spot. You have to make good with Frank because the other teachers who failed with him are watching you, and your status is at stake. Your patience with him is actually an extension of your pride and desire for success, and not of your love for him. Your whole focus is on Frank as a problem child; in truth, Frank has a problem teacher!' "

The next week Nancy met with Frank's parents. They were professional people; the father a college professor and the mother a former teacher. The principal knew that they were quite capable of grasping her problem with the boy, but she did not know for certain whether his behavior at home was as bad as it was in school. After some small talk, she plunged into the heart of the matter.

"I have failed with your boy," she admitted. "He has been such a problem to us that I planned to ask you to remove him from the school. But in thinking this over I have had a new insight. I see that I have been at fault. I have not really loved him. Will you forgive me? I'd like to try again, for I really want to love him."

Frank's mother's eyes filled with tears and she responded with equal candor. "He is our black sheep. We have four other children—two older and two younger than Frank—and we can relate to all of them easily. But it seems we're always picking on Frank."

The parents and the teacher made a pact: they would lavish love on the boy and see what would happen. At the conclusion of the interview, Nancy felt greatly relieved.

A few days later, the friends with whom Nancy had discussed her problem received this letter:

"Dear Friends, a miracle has happened! Frank is already different. When he walked into school on Monday morning my heart did a somersault because I was so glad to see him. I didn't do anything different from other days; in fact, I actually spent less time with him than usual. But what a change, both in my attitude and in his behavior! Whenever my eyes met his I would smile reassuringly and approvingly. His response in courteous behavior was almost unbelievable. I could hardly wait to phone his parents after school to ask what they had done or said to him to cause such a radical change. They replied, 'Nothing, except that we loved him and let him know that we did.' "

Some weeks later Frank consented to let his work be displayed on the wall, along with that of the other children. After about two months, he asked if he could take one of his drawings home. It was his first such request. Apparently he was beginning to feel accepted both at school and at home.

Any cursory appraisal of the situation between Frank and Nancy would have put all of the wrong on the child's side. The obvious verdict would have been that he either had to behave better or leave the school. Yet when the principal sought God's wisdom, *she* was the one who felt the need to change.

This is a fundamental—a primary principle: whenever there is barrier to communication, whenever there is a lack of love, God asks us individually to search our hearts and not attack the attitude of the other person. Our prayer must ever be: "Lord, change this situation, beginning with a change in me."

To the world, this kind of prayer is foolishness. The accepted practice is rather to "pass the buck." America wants Russia to act differently; Arab blames Jew for his difficulties;

labor castigates management; white and Negro alike ask that the other change his attitudes first.

This is most immediately apparent at the family level. Can we face these truths: "Wives, you don't have problem husbands; they have problem wives." "Husbands, the trouble with your wives is you." "Parents, you are your children's thorn in the flesh"?

The Gospel is not the story of the desire to change or coerce someone else. It recounts the extent to which God went "to change himself," to relate to us and to make his love known to us—even to the extent of dying on a cross. God himself assumed the primary and heavier demand. If we let this kind of love flood our lives, we will be praying, "It's me, O Lord, standing in the need of . . . change."

Often a parent will keep himself on a pedestal apart from and above his children, his inner thoughts and much of his life unknown to them. He emphasizes obedience and the observance of rules. Mealtime is devoted to discipline and correction. The parent insists on his right to control and dictate.

But perhaps God is asking that he be willing to be broken and contrite, that he say, "How can I change? Where can I begin to listen, to understand, to communicate? Lord, show me where I need to be different."

To come to such a point demands that we rouse ourselves from the inertia that prevents the costly deepening of relationships. Romance gives way too easily to casualness, and exuberance to boredom.

Aaron Chapman worked hard and came home tired, and he had fallen into the habit of being non-communicative with his wife and children. Often he was downright grumpy. But in contacts with friends, he would brighten up and express himself enthusiastically.

One evening a neighbor called to invite the Chapmans to

a bridge party. Aaron, who took the call, shook himself free of apathy and fairly bubbled. "That sounds great! We'd love to come. Thanks a lot, Helen."

When he hung up the telephone his wife murmured, "I wish *my* name were Helen."

Aaron was stung, but he was honest enough to see what was wrong. The time came when he resolved to change, to summon enthusiasm for his family as well as for his friends.

Mrs. Chapman began to find notes tucked under her pillow, or hidden in the coffee canister: "I love you." Soon Aaron was finding similar notes in his lunch bucket. Both partners became fun to live with, and daily life was far more an adventure than a chore.

With the passage of time, people tend to become more and more rigid. There is a kind of arthritis of the soul that removes flexibility and elasticity. As we grow older we want people to conform to our patterns of thought and behavior. We have set habits which not only control us but try to restrain those around us.

This creeping paralysis can only be fought off by a daily dying to self and a constant aliveness to the infilling of Christ's Spirit. There must be a hundred little deaths to our wants and wishes week after week, year after year. It is not merely that God wants to change our behavior, but that he wants to change *us* inside and make us new creatures in him.

A woman in her seventies, taciturn and undemonstrative, who had rarely reached out to touch people in any way, became aware of this rigidity in herself and determined to do something about it. One Sunday as she prayed during the church service, she felt impelled to put her arm around the woman next to her. During the closing hymn, she did so. When the service was over, her neighbor turned to her with a radiant face and said, "How did you know I needed a touch of friendship this morning? You just *made* that service for me!"

Sad, how often we want to use and manipulate people for our purposes! But God demands that we recognize and honor their personhood. Because we are human, and therefore fallible, it is difficult to see the individual as distinct from his role in life; yet experience shows that man fulfills his role best when he is treated as an individual.

Take the case of a pitcher in a baseball club. He is a person, and he is also part of a team. His manager, of course, views the pitcher in his role, as one cog in a well-oiled machine, and tends to think of him in terms of his function: to pitch well and win games.

But if the manager is wise, he will know how vital it is to respect the personhood of the pitcher. When the player begins to lose control, when runs are scored against him and the bases are loaded, the manager will want him to know that he believes in his ability to get out of the jam. Therefore, instead of replacing him, he will leave him in the game. And how frequently we have seen such a pitcher respond to the faith shown in him. He reaches down into his inner resources and does a superb piece of "clutch pitching." To treat a player only as a means to win the game, and never to see him as a person with hidden potential, is to undermine his confidence and his dignity as a person.

The parallel in a wide variety of situations is apparent, but all too frequently ignored. Parents treat their children as extensions of their own personalities and attitudes, and not as people in their own right. Employers see their workmen as tools to increase production. A pastor looks on his growing congregation as a symbol of his own success.

Christ always saw people as persons. And he asks us to change so that we too will see people as persons toward whom we will constantly take the initiative of building bridges of understanding and assume the burden of responsibility for healing broken relationships and bridging the chasms of loneliness. We all have a great need for love and approval. We long for recognition and rewards. If these things are denied us, we are likely to react with open rebellion. with secretive dishonesty, or with flamboyant bids for attention.

This is particularly true of young people. Harold Peterson, for example, is a youngster who simply cannot please his parents. He is overweight and clumsy, but he sincerely wants to help others and to do his part at home. Unfortunately, he also has periods of listlessness. He always seems to do his work awkwardly. He is forever dropping things.

Harold's parents pressure him mercilessly. They rarely attempt to understand him, to see his point of view, or to sense his deep needs. The boy has a tremendous struggle to be true to his church vows, to love his parents, and, indeed, to love himself. He is tempted to rebel against his childhood training and to break all restraining bonds.

Will the parents redouble the pressure for obedience and conformity, step up their nagging, and intensify the boy's self-consciousness and inferiority? Or will they hear God telling them that the burden of change is on them and not on their son?

Adults are equally familiar with the loneliness of depersonalization. Betty Huston was a graduate of one of America's leading nursing schools. She had been in charge of an operating room, and later had served as assistant superintendent of nurses in a large hospital.

Betty volunteered to go to Africa, where she helped to establish a nurses' training school and gave to many young women an enthusiasm for their calling. Then she was called home because of her father's illness, and for several years until his death Betty nursed him lovingly. When she returned to Africa, the mood of the country had changed. Nationalism had taken over. Native girls were in positions of authority in the hospital. Now Betty was given menial work usually assigned to beginners. She took orders from the very girls she had trained.

At first she resented this bitterly, but slowly the love of Christ who "came among us as one who serves" won out in her heart. She rejoiced to see radiance and fulfillment in the lives of young people around her. A deep bond of friendship was forged between the nurses, regardless of their position or color.

Christians see in Jesus one who could have been depersonalized but who refused to let go of his inner sense of worth and purpose. He did even a slave's work with kingly grace.

We read, "Jesus, knowing that the Father had given all things into his hands, and that he had come from God and was going to God, rose from supper, laid aside his garments . . . . and began to wash the disciples' feet" (John 13:3-5). The opening words of this passage are like a majestic introduction in a symphony when the theme is about to be announced.

Jesus, endowed with all power, conscious of his heavenly origin and of his dedication to fulfill his mission and to return victoriously to God, *began to wash the disciples' feet!* He, the most sublime and the most human of men, placed himself in a position where his humanity could have been lost in servitude. This is true divinity.

Pete and Arlene Mueller have been married for many years. Early in their marriage they were united in many interests, including especially a concern for Christ's Kingdom and a deep love for the Church.

Then a change came over Arlene. She completely lost interest in spiritual values and withdrew from church membership. The attitude she adopted with Pete was, "You live your life and I'll live mine."

Pete couldn't understand it. In his zeal to change Arlene back to her former condition, he made every mistake in the book. For several years he tried pressuring her to go to church, pointing out the bad influence on the children of religious neglect. He spoke of her duty, of what the neighbors would think. He called on her to be true to her childhood training and to her church membership vows. All he ever got in return was an argument or the brush-off.

But now, for seven or eight years, he has seen the mistake of pressure, and sought to set Arlene free, to love her and enjoy her for her own sake. Arlene has many good qualities, and Pete once more sees and appreciates them. He has stopped arguing with her about "spoiling" the children with overindulgence. He has stopped scolding when she stays out late playing bridge with "the girls."

Pete is seeking to go "all the way" in a daily, joyous love toward his children. Often, of course, he slips, but he always apologizes and begins again. He longs for Arlene to rejoin him in dedication to Christ, and many times he prays, "Lord, how long?" He can't understand what is wrong with him. Is his witness so poor that it only stiffens Arlene's resistance to Christ and the Church?

But a recent insight has made a great difference to Pete. Not long ago he came to the place where he saw that his commitment to Christ must be *regardless of what anyone else did*. He saw that he had been thinking in terms of a fifty-fifty arrangement: he would go half way if Arlene would go the other half.

Since then he has seen new areas in which to set his family free. He has found greater joy in loving them for what they are, not for what they might become. He has learned to "roll with the punches," taking rebuffs with good humor while holding firm to his resolve to do God's will as he sees it.

Occasionally he asks himself, "When will my wife change and become a partner with me?" The answer is, "I don't know, and in a sense that is not my concern. My job is to love her, enjoy her, and be the finest husband and father that I can be. If God wants to change Arlene, he will. Meanwhile, I think she's the finest girl in the world, and I'm glad I married her."

Only the power of God can free us so that our actions are not conditioned by the behavior of other people but by the love of Christ. To react to others is to let them control us and determine our moods and courses of action. To be committed to Christ and filled with his love is to let the Master chart our desires and behavior as we respond to him. Difficult? Yes, but possible when we give ourselves to him and let him do in and through us what we cannot do ourselves.

Some people know the joy of companionship and deep fellowship in a home, or with friends. This is truly a wonderful, God-given privilege. Others find that they are called to travel a lonely road, living with people who make things difficult for them even as they profess to love them.

Again and again the miracle of God's friendship enters the lives of those who travel this lonely road. God wants to get us to the place where we love him for himself alone, regardless of what anyone else may say or do. When our commitment is on this unconditional basis, there is an inflow of his Spirit that supersedes and eclipses all other desires. There may still be a poignant, wistful wish for spiritual comradeship, but this is caught up in the joy of God's love and in the faith that ultimately "all things will work together for good."

QUESTIONS FOR DISCUSSION

1. Where should apologies begin? How?
2. What habits hinder spiritual growth? What habits foster it?
3. Whom do you like most to be with? Why?
4. Are you fun to live with?